napa bulletin 8

Negotiating Ethnicity: The Impact of Anthropological Theory and Practice

■ Susan Emley Keefe, ed.

National Association for the Practice of Anthropology
A Unit of the American Anthropological Association

NAPA Bulletins are occasional publications of the National Association for the Practice of Anthropology, a Unit of the American Anthropological Association.

Ralph J. Bishop and Pamela Amoss
General Editors

Library of Congress Cataloging-in-Publication Data

Negotiating ethnicity.

(NAPA bulletin ; 8)
Includes bibliographies.
1. Ethnicity. 2. Ethnology—Methodology.
I. Keefe, Susan E. (Susan Emley) II. Series.
GN495.6.N44 1989 305.8 89-15008
ISBN 0-913167-32-0

ISBN 0-913167-32-0

Contents

Introduction

Susan Emley Keefe

Practicing anthropologists work in a politically charged public arena. The groups with whom they work are frequently ethnic minorities differing culturally and socioeconomically from the mainstream. In this kind of practice, anthropologists necessarily may be called upon to define these ethnic groups, analyze their change through time, and mediate between various groups vying for resources. This requires both a grasp of the theoretical issues concerning the concept of ethnicity and possession of the political skills and sensitivity to deal with group competition and conflict. It also requires practitioners, who may be asked to side with one or another group competing for resources, to consider questions of ethical responsibility. Perhaps most significantly for individuals, it can create special problems and stress in their personal lives as they are called upon to make judgments or intervene in hotly contested decisions. This *Bulletin* is not meant to be definitive on these subjects. Rather, it is intended to initiate more extensive discussion of these issues which generally go unaddressed in the literature on applied anthropology.

As is clear in most theoretical reviews, there is little agreement on a single definition of the concept of ethnicity (Despres 1975; Reminick 1983; Royce 1982). Instead, what emerges is the complex, multidimensional nature of ethnicity and the significance of the social and cultural context in shaping ethnic groups. For example, while ethnicity is generally recognized as based on descent, ethnic groups in practice often develop more through social or political convenience than by blood descent. As another example, ethnicity is commonly defined as having a cultural dimension, yet the *perception* of cultural difference may have greater impact than any objective differences in the life experience of ethnic group members.

In this introduction, I avoid the typical laundry list approach to attributes constituting ethnicity. As an alternative, I will briefly describe three theoretical perspectives which can be usefully adopted in the examination of issues involving ethnicity. These perspectives tend to see ethnicity primarily in terms of the following: process, perception, or empirical phenomena. The processual perspective views ethnicity as a dynamic concept emerging through the negotiation of identities by groups and individuals in a social context. The perspective involving perception is concerned with the meanings attached by groups and individuals to themselves and others and the impact these meanings have on subsequent actions. The empirical phenomena perspective establishes objective ethnic categories and measures the patterns of difference between groups and individuals.

Each of the three case studies following this introduction is developed along the lines of one of these perspectives, although each chapter also addresses elements of all three perspectives. Clearly, multiple theoretical perspectives enhance the understanding of ethnic groups in social context. At the same time, Gilbert points out in the fourth article, practicing anthropologists must be equally concerned with producing "detailed and concrete data" about specific ethnic groups that might be useful to service providers working daily with ethnically diverse clients. This dual concern with theoretical orientation and data collection is essential for the development of effective strategies for practicing anthropology in multiethnic contexts.

Ethnicity and Process

Concern with the concept of ethnic identification has brought about considerable research in the last twenty years focused on the role of intergroup contact and interaction in creating and reinforcing group boundaries as well as group identity (e.g., Barth 1969; Nagata 1974). O'Connor describes a fascinating case for us in which contemporary Chumash ethnicity is created and reinforced primarily in response to state and national environmental legislation and the review process.

Studies of other indigenous groups with small numbers or complex mixed descent frequently note the significance of negotiations with public agencies (such as the BIA), state and federal levels of government, and constituents of neighboring ethnic groups in the establishment of social identity. Blu (1980), for example, describes the historical struggle of the Lumbee, a mixed descent group (black, white, and Indian) in eastern North Carolina, and their attempts to establish the acceptance of an identity first, unsuccessfully, as white and now as Native American—the attainment of federal designation as an official tribe being crucial to the latter. In an international context, the recent attempts by newer nations to seek repatriation of plundered artifacts from former colonial governments can also be interpreted as a means of negotiating for independent cultural legitimacy, higher status, and the right to participate as equals in international politics (Handler 1988).

The movement to adopt the term "African American" as an identifier among black Americans reflects this contemporary concern with ethnic identification and its social and political significance. Whereas the term "black" emphasizes race, color, and the contrast with "white," "African American" signifies a common geographic or national origin, cultural heritage, and independent ethnic status. "Black" is derived from an adjective and denotes a category, while "African American" implies a social group with a common identity.

Perhaps the best example of the significance of the negotiation of ethnicity in the United States is found in the Bureau of the Census. The agency has been reckoning the country's racial and ethnic makeup since 1790, yet no single set of race categories has been used in more than two censuses, and most were used only once. In 1980, three race and ethnic questions were asked, including questions on race, Spanish/Hispanic origin, and (on the long form going to 1/6 of the population) ancestry or national origin. Revised versions of these are planned for the 1990 census.

The U.S. Bureau of the Census recognizes that race is less an objective scientific classification system than it is a set of social categories with political implications (Martin, DeMaio, and Campanelli 1987). Those groups specially designated in the race and Hispanic origin questions are likely to have higher counts than nonlisted subgroups, which means greater political clout and more government funding. This results in intense lobbying by ethnic groups to be listed in the census questions (*The Seattle Times* 1989). In 1980, the list of races included White, Black or Negro, Japanese, Chinese, Filipino, Korean, Vietnamese, Indian (American—specify tribe), Asian Indian, Hawaiian, Guamanian, Samoan, Eskimo, Aleut, and Other (specify). The proposed 1990 list has been shortened to White, Black or Negro, Eskimo, Aleut, Asian or Pacific Islander (specify group), Indian (American—specify tribe), and Other race. Asian subgroups have protested the absence of formal subcounts, in part because the resulting handcounts delay their population enumeration by five years.

The Hispanic origin item was included in the census for the first time in 1970 on the long form due to pressure from the Hispanic community. In 1980 the item was asked of everyone on the short census form. Measurement of Hispanicity has posed considerable problems for the agency for many reasons. For example, there are cultural differences between U.S. Americans and Latin Americans in the definition of racial categories; U.S. Americans are primarily interested in distinguishing between black and white, while Latin Americans generally categorize race in more diverse ways and frequently respond as "other" to the race question (Martin, DeMaio, and Campanelli 1987). Furthermore, Hispanics (particularly those in middle-income levels) often are uncomfortable with minority status labels and choose not to self-identify as Hispanics. The diversity of Hispanic labels and the movement toward new or more encompassing labels (e.g., Latino, Hispanic) that do not specify national origin have contributed to the elimination of official subcounts on the Hispanic origin census question for 1990 (Estrada 1988).

Ethnicity and Perception

Coinciding with recent trends in cultural anthropology has been an interest in the role of perception and the manipulation of symbols in issues of ethnicity. Handler explores the depiction of black Americans at Colonial Williamsburg and, in the process, the role of the museum in defining humanness and the "Other," in depicting ethnic homogeneity versus diversity, and in contributing to an understanding of social systems and their differential impact on groups of people as opposed to cultural materials and their use by individuals.

As Handler points out, museums display property, which is proof of existence and worth in the Western tradition, but the challenge for museums is to examine this and other conceptualizations of being "cultured" or "human." It would seem that the issue of *human* property—slaves—might provide the perfect vehicle to begin such an undertaking. However, as Handler's discussion reveals, both blacks and whites are uncomfortable with the history of slavery. Certainly the issue of slavery would seem crucial to personal identity and status among black Americans. How is it possible to take a painful history of exploitation and turn it into a celebration of peoplehood, of strength and fortitude? The recent occurrence of a reunion of hundreds of descendents of slaves on the grounds of their ancestors' former plantation in North Carolina demonstrates the potential for the development of such a perspective (*Charlotte Observer* 1986).

Claims regarding the ownership of human remains also have implications for museums and conceptualizations of the humanness of others. Egyptian mummies are commonly displayed without protest. Yet indigenous minorities have been successful in provoking public concern regarding a more respectful approach to the retention and display of human remains, particularly those of previously subordinated peoples. One of the most recent cases to receive international attention was the withdrawal for sale of a preserved and tatooed head of a Maori warrior (possibly a slave) from Bonham's, a London auction house (Benthall 1988). The case created considerable publicity and was accompanied by generally sympathetic treatment by the press. Legal action served the "political aspirations" of the Maori and the head was returned to New Zealand for burial due to the efforts of Survival International, an advocate group for tribal rights.

As an editorial in *Anthropology Today* points out, auctioneers in Britain have belatedly responded to the ethical concerns regarding the handling of human remains, while museum curators generally have taken steps already to keep relics out of sight (Benthall 1988). Legislation prohibiting the sale of human remains has been enacted in several states in the United States, and the first arrest of a major dealer in Native American antiquities was made recently in North Carolina (*Charlotte Observer* 1988). Such legislation is of special concern to archeologists because it imposes sanctions on pothunters who destroy archeological sites. However, it also raised questions about the claim archeologists have over human remains in the name of science. It is not inconceivable that one day we might find cultural anthropologists sympathetic to native people's rights at odds with archeologists concerned with scientific data gathering. These are obviously ethical dilemmas of genuine importance to anthropologists of all persuasions, and questions which practicing anthropologists can and should establish leadership in resolving.

Ethnicity and Empirical Phenomena

More traditional as an approach to the study of ethnicity has been the measurement of traits and patterns of difference between ethnic groups. Such studies tend to focus on groups commonly accepted as ethnic by self-identity and/or forced identity. Keefe, Reck, and Reck approach the concept of ethnicity from a theoretical perspective and set out to test their model on a group whose ethnicity has been questioned—white Southern Appalachians. In the process of applying objective measures of ethnicity (demonstrating statistical significance in the end), they are struck by the importance of the "social context" or, in their case, great numbers of people who are angry that they have been forced to confront overtly the otherwise covert sociocultural barriers and limitations in their lives. The experience of Keefe, Reck, and Reck illustrates the salience each of the three perspectives reviewed in this introduction can contribute to the understanding of any single ethnic situation. Regarding white Southern Appalachians, while certain cultural differences do set them apart from mainstream Americans, it is the negotiation of individual status and identity which is more significant in determining the boundaries of the ethnic group. Moreover, those group boundaries are fluid and shift in response to new goals and issues as they arise.

As imprecise as categories of objective measurement of ethnicity might be, given the importance of social change and the perceptual differences, objective categories nevertheless facilitate the analysis of patterns of difference between groups. Thus, in the county in western North Carolina studied by Keefe, Reck, and Reck, those students most prone to do poorly in or to drop out of school are those of Appalachian descent while non-Appalachian in-migrants tend to do well academically, and differences in culture, identity, social class, and rural versus urban residence all contribute in a systematic way to this societal condition.

Gilbert's argument that service providers, planners, and policymakers require hard data based on standardized groups takes on special significance here. Given the demand for culturally relevant services, practitioners must have factual information relevant for better meeting the real needs of people from various ethnic groups in their everyday life. Applied anthropologists doing research must continue to work toward clarifying theoretical concepts and applying measurement to their analysis in order to provide the kind of data useful in practice.

As a standardized category of analysis, race has virtually disappeared from anthropological discourse following extended criticism of its scientific basis in the 1940s and '50s. Physical anthropologists subsequently turned to the study of specific biological adaptations. It is interesting to note, however, that the primary anthropological field to retain race as an empirical concept is the applied field of forensic anthropology. This is the result of the need for scales of measurement which facilitate the social and biological identification of skeletal remains. The Giles and Elliot (1962) formulas, for example, differentiate between blacks, whites, and Indians on several cranial measurements. Of course, in these formulas, race is used quite properly as a statistical category.

In cultural anthropology, interest began to turn at this time from race (or tribe) to the concept of ethnicity based on the cultural definition of groups. Although physical attributes may have been incorporated into definitions of ethnic groups, they never became the focus of particular study. Yet, recent research indicates that physical attributes are significantly correlated with social and cultural characteristics within ethnic groups. For example, in an analysis of a national Chicano survey of almost 1000 respondents, Arce, Murguia, and Frisbie (1987) found that Mexican Americans with darker skin color and more "Indian-looking" features were significantly lower in socioeconomic status and more likely to use the Spanish language and self-identify with their ethnic descent group than lighter skinned, "European-looking" Mexican Americans. For Chicanos and blacks, there is also the tendency within the ethnic group to judge those with lighter skin color as more attractive.

In sum, the role played by physical attributes in establishing markers of and variation in ethnicity would appear to deserve greater attention. In what ways, for example, is ethnic identity and group formation dependent upon physical differences? Is ethnicity in the United States differently constituted among peoples who are indistinguishable physically from the mainstream (e.g., white Southern Appalachians) as opposed to people of color? Is there less tendency or ability to come together as a political interest group without a clear physical marker of identity? Is there less need for culturally relevant services among these groups? For applied anthropologists, who tend to value equitable access to social benefits but also tend to be confined by governmental definitions of ethnicity, these should become important questions for research and practice.

General Implications for Future Practice

Applied anthropologists, as Chambers (1986) and Van Willigen (1986) have emphasized, are involved in social change and group activity directed toward goals. Ethnicity is often considered a static, descriptive variable insufficient for the formulation of programs of deliberate change (Chambers 1986). In this *Bulletin,* a multidimensional approach to ethnicity is offered in order to provide useful alternatives for practitioners trying to interpret group behavior and formulate and implement relevant policy. Anthropologists have important roles in both the discussion of basic assumptions regarding the nature of human communities and the application of knowledge in applied contexts. Applied anthropologists should ' in the forefront of the continuing dialogue concerning ethnicity as a c cept useful in theory and practice.

While various theoretical perspectives can be employed in the context of practicing anthropology, it is also recognized that government agencies, legal systems, and policymakers require concrete definitions of ethnic groups for the measurement of segments of the population and appropriate distribution of resources. Moreover, practitioners and planners must have specific information on ethnic group members' beliefs and behavior in order to assess needs within the group and develop culturally relevant services. Practicing anthropologists are perhaps uniquely qualified both to apply various theoretical models in the study of ethnic groups and then to develop the most equitable programs of action. Given a complex multiethnic society, it will be increasingly important to develop ethical standards for dealing with situations in which ethnic groups and subgroups compete for anthropological legitimacy as a means of bolstering their political claims. Practicing anthropologists might also be encouraged to share relevant experiences involving personal and professional emotional trauma, thereby contributing to a more informed expectation for and ability to manage ethnic group conflict in the applied arena.

Note

Acknowledgment. I would like to thank Leslie Brownrigg and Napio McKinney for their assistance in providing information on the definition of race and ethnicity by the U.S. Bureau of the Census.

References Cited

Arce, Carlos, Edward Murguia, and W. Parker Frisbie
1987 Phenotype and Life Chances among Chicanos. Hispanic Journal of Behavioral Sciences 9:19–32.
Barth, Fredrik, ed.
1969 Ethnic Groups and Boundaries. Boston: Little, Brown and Co.
Benthall, Jonathan
1988 The Bonham's Head Affair. Anthropology Today 4:1–2.
Blu, Karen
1980 The Lumbee Problem: The Making of an American Indian People. Cambridge: Cambridge University Press.
Chambers, Erve
1986 Applied Anthropology: A Practical Guide. Englewood Cliffs, NJ: Prentice-Hall.
Charlotte Observer
1986 Slave Descendant's Reunion: Families Gather at N.C. Plantation. Saturday, August 30, p. 1F.
1988 Antiquities Dealer Charged. Thursday, October 20, p. 1C.
Despres, Leo A.
1975 Toward a Theory of Ethnic Phenomena. *In* Ethnicity and Resource Competition in Plural Society. Leo A. Despres, ed. The Hague: Mouton.
Estrada, Leobardo
1988 Ethnic Self-Identification and Labeling: Consequences of Acculturation. Keynote address at the Second Symposium on Ethnic Identity: Family Influences on Hispanic Ethnic Identity, Tempe, AZ, April 28.
Giles, E., and O. Elliot
1962 Race Identification from Cranial Measurements. Journal of Forensic Sciences 7:147–156.
Handler, Richard
1988 Culture Wars: National Identity and the "Repatriation" of Heritage. Paper presented at the annual meeting of the American Anthropological Association, Chicago, December 21.

Martin, Elizabeth, Theresa J. DeMaio, and Pamela C. Campanelli
1987 Context Effects for Census Measures of Race and Hispanic Origin. *In* 1990 Planning Conference Series, No. 12, Race and Ethnic Items. Washington, D.C.: U.S. Bureau of the Census.
Nagata, Judith A.
1974 What is a Malay? Situational Selection of Ethnic Identity in a Plural Society. American Ethnologist 1.331–350.
Reminick, Ronald A.
1983 Theory of Ethnicity: An Anthropologist's Perspective. Lanham, MD: University Press of America.
Royce, Anya Peterson
1982 Ethnic Identity: Strategies of Diversity. Bloomington: Indiana University Press.
The Seattle Times
1989 Racial Realities: The Coming Census Illustrates the Pitfalls of Pigeonholing People by Ethnic Origin. Sunday, January 15, p. 1
Van Willigen, John
1986 Applied Anthropology: An Introduction. South Hadley, MA: Bergin and Garvey.

Environmental Impact Review and the Construction of Contemporary Chumash Ethnicity

Mary I. O'Connor

In October of 1986, three human skeletons were unearthed during the course of the routine laying of utility lines in Santa Barbara, California. These remains were given to the county coroner, who determined that they were probably from a prehistoric Indian burial. The skeletons were turned over to a physical anthropologist at the local university for final determination of their antiquity.[1] State law requires that, after analysis, such remains be given to the most likely nearest kin descended from the individuals whose remains were uncovered (State of California 1982). The Native American Heritage Commission, also set up by state law (State of California 1982), has appointed one person to be in charge of reburying Indian remains found along the Santa Barbara coast and inland as well as on the Santa Barbara Channel Islands. This is the area formerly inhabited by the Chumash Indians and their predecessors.[2]

The Heritage Commission appointee, having heard of the find, contacted the physical anthropologist and asked him to turn over the skeletons. Soon afterwards, the anthropologist was contacted by a group of people claiming to be the descendants of residents of the Chumash village located on the site where the burials were found. These people insisted that the Native American Heritage Commission appointee was not only not descended from that village, but not even of Chumash descent. Despite the fact that everyone involved in the dispute knew that this was indeed the case, the remains were ultimately turned over to the non-Chumash individual for reburial.

How can it be that a person whose descent is known to be other than Chumash should adamantly insist on his Chumash identity? Why is it that in this case and many others, individuals who only claim Chumash identity routinely win out over those whose Chumash ancestry can be traced to Spanish mission records? Perhaps most important, why do so many people care so much about these issues? The case of the three skeletons is only one of the latest episodes in a 20-year story of emerging ethnicity, developing environmental law, and shifting coalitions among a variety of local groups, all of whom claim Chumash ethnicity.

Issues in the Practice of Anthropology

My participation in the analysis of impacts to Native American concerns in the Santa Barbara area began in 1980 and has always been intermittent. I was the principal investigator on the Chevron Oil Company pipeline project and on many other smaller projects. Over the years, I have become aware of some of the problems, both professional and personal, involved in environmental impact report work.

One professional problem involves the decision to do such work at all. On one hand, the wages are quite high, although there is no job security and the work is very stressful. On the other hand, there is the ethical problem of participating in a system that rewards one group while essentially ignoring others. It is also necessary to consider the fact that, given the high pay and general lack of outside review by qualified professionals, there is often the tendency for ethnographers to do "quick and dirty" work; this tendency is exacerbated by the process of granting contracts to the lowest bidder.

Given the lack of any real guidelines for conducting research on Native American concerns, I had to establish research methods that would comply with the relevant laws, produce a statement representing the views of all relevant groups, and preserve my personal and professional integrity. These matters are at times very difficult to reconcile. While I still have qualms about working on environmental impact reports, I feel that by carefully practicing the traditional methods of key informant interviews, participant observation, and archival research, it is possible for practitioners to produce a report that does justice to all concerned. The lack of impartiality and the tendency for ethnographers to favor one group over the others, as well as the tendency to ignore traditional field methods in favor of copying other environmental impact reports, are two problems encountered frequently in the field.

Another professional problem involved in this work in the Santa Barbara area is the ongoing disagreement between archeologists and Native Americans about who should be allowed to excavate sites and what the ultimate disposition of artifacts should be. This issue of burials has been established by state law: the Indians are to rebury any remains affected during development. Which Indians, as I have indicated, is another matter. Beyond burials, the question of the artifacts is an issue of great debate. The archeologists believe they should have them for research. The Indians feel they should have them because they were made by their ancestors. In this debate, the ethnographer is constantly asked to side with one group or another.

I have carefully sidestepped this issue by not taking sides. However, many authors of environmental impact reports do side with one group or the other, thereby jeopardizing the research outcomes and, at times, their own health and safety. In the Santa Barbara area, the stakes are very high for this kind of work, and so is the rate of stress. Because of the high wages, people are tempted to take the work. However, because of the stress involved, the work is at best short-term, or for short periods over a long career. The personal stress comes from the need to submit competitive bids, the lack of job security, and the difficulty of dealing with groups who are permanently hostile to each other.

A final issue for the practice of anthropology in this context is relating theory to practice. Readers of environmental impact reports are not interested in anthropological theory. They are interested in complying with state and federal laws. At the same time, no one is likely to dedicate a long-term project to the contemporary "Chumash," simply because they are so few and there are few, if any, cultural elements left. As a result, some theoretical findings have gone unpublished until now. This article is the product of many projects conducted over the course of five years. Thus, it has been possible to conduct applied anthropology and also to present a theoretical conclusion that contributes to the existing body of theory.

The Emergence of Chumash Ethnicity

One of the major theoretical debates over ethnicity concerns the extent of cultural content involved in ethnic identity. The primordialist view, at one extreme, contends that language, religion and values, in addition to race and other circumstances of birth, are essential elements of ethnicity (Shils 1957; Geertz 1963; Spicer 1971; Castile and Kushner 1981). At the other extreme of the vast continuum of theoretical views on this topic is the position that ethnic identity is based on competition for resources—economic and/or political—from outside the ethnic group (Barth 1969; Benedict 1962).

The case of the Chumash demonstrates the power of outside resources to actually construct an ethnic entity where there had been none before. Competition for external political and economic resources has taken place among the various shifting groups and coalitions that have since emerged. Although the people expressing Chumash ethnicity often refer to the importance of Chumash religion and other values in their lives, in fact they learned of these cultural elements as adults from anthropologists. Thus, Chumash ethnic identity is based almost entirely on outside stimuli. Although some people can demonstrate Chumash descent, others who cannot are recognized by political authorities and by developers. Ironically, those who can prove descent are often the least likely to express Chumash ethnicity in the context of the environmental review process.

The story begins in 1968, with the formation of the Quabajai Chumash Indian Association. This group was made up of several different individuals and groups, all presumed to be of Chumash ancestry, none of whose decent had been formally established. Members of the Santa Ynez Indian Reservation had the most sound basis for claiming Chumash ancestry, as Reservation members must prove one-quarter Indian descent. Other founding members, notably a large extended family, had been told by their parents and grandparents that they had Indian or Chumash blood. This loose coalition came into being in response to the U.S. government's 1968 decision to reopen the federal Indian rolls. The new law stipulated that anyone who could establish California Indian ancestry would be eligible to receive cash payments as well as other benefits (P.L. 90-507, 82 Stat. 860).

Beginning in 1969, Native American archeological sites came under the protection of a series of federal and California state law. Together these laws provided for a long, complex process of environmental review before any development project could be approved. The legal protection of archeological sites provided a rallying point for the expression of Native American identity. At the same time, there was a nationwide revival of Indian activism, which in turn coincided with the passage of laws protecting Native American religious freedom and other aspects of Indian life.

The conjunction of concerns over Native American rights and over the environment was a crucial step in the construction of Chumash ethnicity in the Santa Barbara area. Also crucial to this emergence was the fact that the Santa Barbara region contains hundreds and perhaps thousands of archeological sites. Because many of the sites are located in prime real estate areas, the Indians became one element of a complex mix of groups opposed to development. The first major battle featuring this coalition occurred in 1977 over Hammond's Meadow.

Hammond's Meadow: The First Battleground

Hammond's Meadow is a valuable piece of property overlooking the Pacific Ocean in the exclusive community of Montecito. In March 1977, the owners of the property announced that they were preparing a development plan for the land. In 1978, the preliminary environmental impact report on Hammond's Meadow became available to the public. The archeology section of this document stated that the archeological site on the parcel was possibly a part of the historic Chumash village of Shalwaj. The archeologists felt that sufficient protection of the site could be built into the project through various means. However, a representative of the Quabajai Association stated that no matter what precautions were taken, there would be major destruction of the site as an aspect of Chumash heritage (*Santa Barbara News-Press* 1978).

Beginning with the Hammond's Meadow project, the environmental review process in Santa Barbara became the focus for the expression of pride in a Chumash identity which was newly imbued with prestige as well as with influence on local politicians. This influence came increasingly under the control of a single large extended family that was among the founding members of the Quabajai. This family, which I will call Family A, became very adept at gaining the ear of public officials and even, in some cases, of the developers themselves.

Point Concepcion: The Consolidation of Ethnicity

If Hammond's Meadow represents the birth of political activity by people claiming Chumash descent, the Point Concepcion Liquified Natural

Gas proposal provided a locus for the flowering of Chumash ethnicity in the Santa Barbara area. In 1977, Southern California Edison proposed the construction of a liquified natural gas (LNG) processing facility at Point Concepcion, a remote spot at the extreme western end of Santa Barbara County. Bolstered by their success so far in influencing the course of the Hammond's Meadow review process, the Quabajai Association looked at the Point Concepcion project as another matter on which to make their voices heard. The point itself has no known archeological sites, but has been identified as the Chumash "Western Gate," the place where souls of the dead pass into the spirit world (Blackburn 1975:98). The Quabajai Association seized upon the religious significance of the point and, by association, an extensive area around it, as the basis for their protest. In May of 1978, in response to concerns about the possibility of earthquake faults at the site, trenching for evidence of faults began. On May 10, Point Concepcion was occupied by members of the Quabajai Association, who insisted that they would remain at the site until the bulldozers left. They cited the recently passed Native American Heritage Act as the basis for their action, stating that the act prohibits severe and irreparable damage to designated types of sacred sites.

The encampment at Point Concepcion lasted from May 1978 until March 1979. This period was very important for the development and consolidation of Chumash ethnicity. The geographical isolation and great natural beauty of the location, the intensity of daily interaction among a small number of people, and the dedication and commitment of those people to a well-defined cause all combined to create the conditions under which social movements tend to develop and flourish (Erasmus 1977:135–179). To this day, participants look back with nostalgia at what they perceive as a period of Native American solidarity.

The Point Concepcion encampment was ended by a court order in March of 1979. Over a period of several years, suits and countersuits were filed over the proposed terminal, with no firm decision until July of 1987. At that time, a state assembly bill blocking the LNG terminal was signed into law by the governor (*Santa Barbara News-Press* 1987).

The Aftermath of Point Concepcion

In the years following the Point Concepcion encampment, the Native American community underwent several important changes. A variety of groups with different goals and lifestyles developed out of the existing Quabajai Association. Some families broke off from the Quabajai because they became disaffected with Family A. These families and others eventually formed the Santa Barbara Indian Center, the Cieneguitas Indian Association, and several other groups. The Santa Ynez Indian Reservation withdrew from the Quabajai because of political disagreements over the goals of the Association. The outcome of this process was that the Quabajai was reduced to members of Family A.

In order to preserve some of the solidarity lost by the splintering of the Quabajai, the splinter groups banded together to form the United Chumash Council. Each group, including the Quabajai Association, was to have a representative on the Council, which was to meet regularly. Eventually, all of the groups except a remnant of the original Quabajai withdrew from the Council, leaving Family A as the sole members. The United Chumash Council nevertheless continued to represent itself as the arbiter of Native American concerns in the county.

One of the issues that became important after Point Concepcion was that of Native American monitors. The guidelines set up to implement the California Environmental Quality Act of 1970 included the provision of archeologists as monitors on projects which might disturb archeological sites. These monitors observe all digging operations and are empowered to stop any project that endangers a site. The United Chumash Council demanded, and eventually got, a county guideline directing that Native American monitors also be present on such projects.

In the period immediately following Point Concepcion, Native American monitors worked for free or were paid wages similar to those paid to workers in archeology laboratories. During this period, members of Family A were the most vocal in pressing the demand for monitors. The Reservation also set up a representative for Native American concerns and sought training for monitors from the Reservation. This and a number of other issues led to a widening gap between the Reservation and non-Reservation members of various Native American groups. The issue of who should be allowed to monitor became paramount, and this matter was finally settled after a number of disputes. The United Chumash Council (i.e., Family A) would provide monitors for projects to the south of the Coastal Range, which bisects the county. The Reservation would provide monitors for projects in the northern part of the county.

While Family A and the Reservation were squabbling over the monitor issue, the Cieneguitas Indian Association, one of the groups that had broken off from the Quabajai, continued the genealogical research that had originally inspired the formation of the Quabajai. The head of Cieneguitas sought the help of a local ethnohistorian and student of mission records in this research. In 1983, based largely on his examination of mission records, the ethnohistorian came to the conclusion that most of the members of the Cieneguitas Association and the principal members of Family A lacked any Chumash ancestry. Nevertheless, Family A and its supporters remained adamant about their Chumash identity. That identity was first seriously challenged in the revival of the Hammond's Meadow project in 1983. In a letter to the county environmental review office on behalf of the developer, an archeologist raised damaging questions as to the Chumash identity of the people protesting the development:

> In a very real way, these groups define their identity by the extent to which their claims are publicly recognized. Hence, participation in development disputes causes significant recognition. [Craig 1983:8]

This, in a nutshell, describes the construction of Chumash ethnicity: the expression of ethnic identity derives almost completely from outside recognition. This recognition comes from local political leaders and developers; it also takes the form of wages for monitoring. The traditional cultural elements of ethnicity, such as language, religion, and values, are absent.

It would seem that the challenges from the ethnohistorian and the archeologist would bring about the eclipse of Family A as a viable representative of Chumash culture, but this did not in fact occur. County officials have repeatedly stated that ethnic descent is not a factor in claims that a site is of concern to Native Americans, thereby continuing the process of constructing Chumash ethnicity. This decision to ignore descent was crucial in the ensuing battle over control of the Chevron pipeline project and, indeed, over the issue of Chumash ethnicity in general.

The Chevron Pipeline: Showdown over Ethnicity

In 1983, a large quantity of oil was discovered off Point Concepcion in Santa Barbara County. Because of the relatively greater possibility of oil spills resulting from tanker transportation, the county negotiated an agreement with the oil companies to have the oil transported by pipeline to its ultimate destination in Texas. Chevron Oil Corporation won the contract to build the coastal section of the pipeline. The fact that the pipeline would come onto land at Point Concepcion was one major prospective concern for Native Americans. An even greater complication became clear when the pipeline route was revealed: the route crossed a large number of archeological sites.

By 1983, the tone of Chumash ethnic expression had changed quite a bit from the heady days of the Point Concepcion encampment. The fervor of the social movement spawned by the encampment had died down somewhat, and the issue of money had become more important to those claiming Chumash descent. Since the agreement on monitors had been reached between the United Chumash Council and the Reservation, this issue seemingly had been resolved. However, there was still a certain amount of tension between those two groups. Chevron upset the delicate balance by agreeing to hire the United Chumash Council exclusively as monitors on the pipeline project, and to pay them $20 to $25 an hour. Given the length of time—several years—that construction would last, and the high probability of a large number of sites being affected, this represented quite a windfall for Family A.

The agreement between Chevron and the United Chumash Council came after a series of meetings between members of Family A, the Reservation Business Council, county officials and myself. During the course of these meetings, the United Chumash Council members repeatedly brought up the boundary established earlier for monitoring; the Reservation members denied the existence of such a boundary. Ultimately, through intimidation and threats of physical violence, the United Chumash Council persuaded the Reservation Business Council to withdraw from the battle. The success of the United Chumash Council in being so recognized by Chevron and, in a way, by the Reservation, provided incentive for the continued expression of Chumash ethicity.

In the course of the initial surveying and excavation of sites along the pipeline route, three historic Chumash villages were identified as possible impact areas by the project. An extended family on the Reservation was identified as descended from one of the villages. This family, which I will call Family B, very quickly understood some of the implications of their ancestry for cultural resource management in the area. Citing their legitimate ties to a coastal village, they challenged the United Chumash Council's monopoly on coastal monitoring. Calling themselves the Elders Council, the Reservation group began to express Chumash ethnicity in the forum of the environmental review process. Although they were too late to get monitoring rights on the Chevron project, they did ultimately get exclusive monitoring rights on the Hammond's Meadow project, which in 1985 was in the final stages of environmental review. The final approval of the much-protested Hammond's Meadow project came in 1986. Members of the Elders Council stated that the project had sufficient safeguards to prevent the disturbance of the archeological site, and this was recorded as the definitive statement of Native American concerns, despite protests and a lawsuit filed by the United Chumash Council.

This was the context of the dispute that I described at the beginning of this article. Members of Family B, citing state law and claiming that they were the descendants of the people in the burial, challenged the Family A member's right to rebury the bones. The fact that the bones were ultimately reburied by the non-Chumash individual indicates that the power of Family A, while somewhat diminished, had by no means disappeared.

Conclusion

The emergence of Chumash ethnicity is the product of the interaction between outside events and the responses to those events by individuals and families in the Santa Barbara area. Individuals expressing Chumash ethnicity have been rewarded in clear ways for their behavior. Beginning in 1968, a series of laws facilitated this behavior and allowed for increasing levels of formal input into the environmental review process. This process, in turn, became the forum for the expression and subsequent recognition of Chumash ethnicity. Those evincing this ethnicity became influential in the decisions of policymakers in the county government. They were also hired as monitors on excavations and development projects. Their economic and political success was an incentive to further ethnic expression. To some primordialists, it might appear fortunate that the group demonstrably Chumash by descent, Family B, has won at least one battle in the environmental wars. However, the fact is that the manifested ethnicity of *both* Family A and Family B is constructed—both arose in response to external stimuli.

Because the development and construction of Chumash ethnicity has been a response to external events, it is likely that the continued expression of this identity will depend heavily on the nature of such events in the future. Given the availability of land for development, the existence of an active environmentalist community, and the precedent established by county officials in the past, it is probable that Chumash ethnicity will continue to be expressed for the foreseeable future in the Santa Barbara area.

Notes

[1]The information in this article is derived from interviews with the principals involved, from newspaper coverage of events referred to, and from my experience as an ethnologist for the environmental review process on numerous projects from 1980 through 1985.

[2]Because of the controversy over ethnicity which is central to the situation described here, certain terms must be identified specifically as to their meaning. *Native American* and *Indian* will be used to describe anyone claiming Indian ancestry of any sort, whether or not it has been verified or recognized by any government agency. *Chumash* will be used to describe the aboriginal inhabitants of the research area and living individuals with verifiable Chumash ancestry. The term *Chumash ethnicity* will be used for the expression of Chumash identity either by those whose ancestors are known to be Chumash or by people seeking recognition as Chumash for various reasons.

References Cited

Barth, Fredrik
1969 Ethnic Groups and Boundaries. Boston: Little, Brown.
Benedict, Burton
1962 Stratification in Plural Societies. American Anthropologist 64:1235–1246.
Blackburn, Thomas
1975 December's Child. Berkeley: University of California Press.
California, State of
1982 Public Resources Code Sect. 5097.9, 5097.94.
Castile, George P., and Gilbert Kushner, eds.
1981 Persistent Peoples. Tucson: University of Arizona Press.
Craig, Stephen
1983 Native American Concerns and the Hammonds Estate, Critique of the Adequacy and Accuracy of the Ocean Meadows EIR (813-EIR-16). County of Santa Barbara, California.
Erasmus, Charles J.
1977 In Search of the Common Good. New York: Free Press.
Geertz, Clifford
1963 The Integrative Revolution. *In* Old Societies and New States. Clifford Geertz, ed. Glencoe, IL: Free Press.
Santa Barbara News-Press
1978 Hearing Set for Hammond's Meadow. August 23, pp. B-1 and 2.
1987 Deukmejian Bars Natural Gas Terminal. July 25, p. A-1
Shils, Edward
1957 Primordial, Personal, Sacred and Civil Ties. British Journal of Sociology June:130–147
Spicer, Edward
1971 Persistent Cultural Systems. Science 174(19):795–800.
U.S. Government
1968 Public Law 90-507, 82 Stat. 860.

Ethnicity in the Museum

Richard Handler

More and more anthropologists now include among their stock of fieldwork anecdotes tales of informants who excuse themselves from interview sessions to consult ethnographies written in prior generations, works understood by the "natives" themselves as authoritative sources for their "traditional" culture. This is a situation that our anthropological ancestors did not, apparently, envision. For example, in the preface to *Witchcraft, Oracles, and Magic Among the Azande,* Evans-Pritchard concludes an expression of gratitude to the Azande by noting that he inscribes his thanks "even though the Azande will never see them in print" (1937:viii). Today few ethnographers could imagine such a situation. To the contrary, we operate in a world in which anthropological knowledge interacts routinely with natives' understanding of their culture, and with their changing conceptions of collective identity.

In this new condition of anthropological work (some have labeled it "post-colonial"), anthropologists are hired as "consultants" by those whom we formerly called "our people." Asked to document and preserve culture, to teach native languages, to write grammars, to provide historical data for ammunition in court cases and political claims, many who would not have considered themselves applied anthropologists have become such after the fact. Our new usefulness perhaps allows us to see ourselves as resources rather than nuisances, but the dependence of natives upon anthropological discourse is as much a manifestation of Western world-domination as the more obviously imperialistic practices of the colonial era.

To put it bluntly: the rest of the world has been persuaded, or forced, to re-imagine itself in the language of Western social science. Not only have we re-invented "the other" as discrete cultures (Wagner 1975), we have made it difficult for them not to do so as well. They must speak the language that power understands.

In this paper, I consider one aspect of this situation—that involving ethnicity in the museum. Ten years ago, Edward Alexander, longtime director of interpretation at Colonial Williamsburg and, later, Director of Museum Studies at the University of Delaware, published a state-of-the-art introduction to museums entitled *Museums in Motion* (1979). At the outset he noted that the exclusion of minority groups from museums had roused trenchant criticisms that museums would have to address. Alexander quoted a black poet, June Jordon, who had "electrified" an audience of museum professionals with the following remarks:

> Take me into the museum and show me myself, show me my people, show me soul America. If you cannot show me myself, if you cannot teach my people what they need to know . . . then why shouldn't I attack the temples of America and blow them up? The people who hold the power, and the people who count pennies, and the people who hold the keys better start thinking it all over again. [1979:6]

Since the late 1970s, much has been done to include minority groups in those mainstream museums of art and history from which their exclusion had, previously, been almost complete. For example, at Colonial Williamsburg, where I have been conducting research since 1986, a movement to include significant representation of "the other half"—that is, the slave population of the colonial capital of Virginia—dates to the late 1970s, and is today an important interpretive focus. Moreover, preliminary research at several other major history museums in the United States indicates that it is today *de rigueur* for each museum to feature exhibitions about a minority group which can be seen as relevant to that segment of the mainstream culture the museum celebrates. Thus, museums once devoted to WASP history and patriotism now include Amerindians, blacks, Hispanics, and where no acceptable ethnic group is available, women and workers. As Colonial Williamsburg's most recent master plan for interpretation, the theme of which is "Becoming Americans," puts it:

> The history we teach at Colonial Williamsburg must . . . explain to visitors how not only English but also African, European, and surviving Indian peoples built separate yet interdependent societies and how each provided its members with creative opportunities to lead lives worth living even in slavery or under cultural domination. [Colonial Williamsburg Foundation 1985:4–5]

From an anthropological perspective, it is difficult to see the inclusion of others' stories in such elite institutions as museums as anything but a step toward greater intercultural understanding. Yet I want to suggest that the construction of those stories in terms of what is today a common-sense—and hegemonic—theory of culture may work against intercultural understanding. The display of ethnic culture in museums reproduces an ideology of culture that homogenizes or domesticates, rather than enhances, cultural diversity. As I have argued elsewhere (Handler 1988), the construction of ethnicity is governed by certain features of modern ideology which ensure that cultural differences are all packaged and marketed in exactly the same way. All ethnic groups come out looking the same: like a row of ethnic restaurants in a modern city, every ethnic group displays its difference by selling its cuisine, but, from another perspective, all become identical because they are all doing the same thing, viz., claiming uniqueness, defined as cuisine (or costume, dance, music, and so on), and then selling that uniqueness in the markets of the consumer society.

The "features of modern ideology" relevant to this argument are epitomized by the term "possessive individualism," taken from C. B. Macpherson's 1962 classic discussion of seventeenth-century English political theory. Briefly, possessive individualism stresses not only the focus of modern Western culture on individual human beings (imagined as complete unto themselves, independent of all social ties), but our understanding of individuals as intimately connected to—indeed, as defined by—the property they possess. In the domain of cultural politics, where national or ethnic groups are understood as "collective individuals" (Dumont 1970), the property that proves the existence of a group is its culture. "We are a nation because we have a culture"—these words of a Quebecois informant (Handler 1985) encapsulate the ideology of most ethnic groups who today strive, worldwide, to prove their existence and worthiness by displaying themselves in museums. The possessive metaphor—to have a culture—is not accidental: in ethnic, museological, and anthropological theories of culture, a group demonstrates its individuality and identity by the possession and display of what is now known as "cultural property." Yet we must ask whether the business of reimagining lives and traditions in hegemonic terms represents the free expression of diversity or, rather, its suppression. The remainder of this paper illustrates these arguments with an ethnographic glance at the development of black history at Colonial Williamsburg. My remarks are based on field observations, interviews, and archival research. Though only one example, the material suggests something of the dilemma that ethnicity in the museum presents to anthropologists, museum professionals, and ethnic activists alike.

Displaying "The Other Half" at Colonial Williamsburg

As is well known, Colonial Williamsburg was the pet project of John D. Rockefeller, Jr. Since its inception in 1926, millions of Rockefeller dollars have been invested in the restoration of the colonial capital of Virginia. The museum today is comprised of more than 500 buildings and employs more than 3,000 people. Though Colonial Williamsburg has always been dedicated to a nationalistic presentation of colonial American history, the interpretive emphasis of the museum has evolved. In the early years of the restoration, architecture and furnishings were stressed, but a patriotic interpretation of the Revolutionary War period was developed in response to World War II and the ensuing cold war. By the early 1960s, the emphasis was broadened to include colonial society as well as political history. This shift continued in the late 1960s and 1970s with the rise of social history followed by the emergence of such specialties as women's history, black history, and ethnohistory. The new stories that these subdisciplines made available interacted with new interpretive and pedagogical techniques, particularly those associated with so-called living history, or the use of third- and, especially, first-person characters to act out historical roles for the public.

Blacks have always been a significant component of Colonial Williamsburg's labor force. In 1952, for example, there were over 600 black employees in a total of 1,363 (Colonial Williamsburg Foundation 1952).

But, as one would expect, they were not distributed evenly throughout the museum organization. They worked as construction laborers, gardeners, custodians, laundresses, maids, bellmen, and waiters, but not in professional or managerial positions, nor as hostesses and escorts to the public. The career trajectories of black employees show that before the 1960s, blacks rarely advanced in the museum's organizational hierarchy. The civil rights movement reached Colonial Williamsburg in the 1960s, and the museum responded by promoting blacks to managerial positions, usually in departments whose personnel were predominantly black. But, as elsewhere in the United States, *de facto* integration has come much more slowly than an overt acceptance of the civil rights ideology.

This sketch of black employment *within* Colonial Williamsburg forms an important backdrop for an account of the portrayal of black culture *by* Colonial Williamsburg. A 1937 *National Geographic* article on the museum features a photograph of two Revolutionary-era soldiers, red-coated and musket-bearing, who smilingly tower over two barefooted black children eating watermelon. The caption reads: "THERE IS ONE CUSTOM THAT TIME HAS NOT CHANGED," and the accompanying text speaks of "pickaninnies . . . up to their ears in watermelon" (Goodwin 1937:418). On the same page another photograph shows an original eighteenth-century coach in use in 1937 and manned by liveried black servants; the caption has no racial content. These costumed servants are typical of how blacks figured in recreated historic scenes before 1979. Though blacks appeared routinely as costumed kitchen helpers, coachmen, and even craftsmen, and black custodial workers in public view also donned colonial costume, there was no discussion of slavery or the black community. As I was told by one official, interpreters were instructed never "to use the word 'slave.' They [blacks] were servants." According to my informant, the NAACP made it known in the late 1950s that it didn't want slavery discussed. The past was, I was told, too painful both for black employees and visitors. No one wanted to dwell historically upon it. As two students of black historiography have recently asked, "What was there to celebrate in reminders of servitude and of an exploitative relationship, the effects of which were still being felt?" (Fraser and Butler 1986:129).

In 1979, the museum organized a "living history" program, creating the Company of Colonial Performers.[1] This group of actors developed colonial characters, or roles, based on historical research. Actors in character strolled through the museum at various times to engage visitors in conversation, or appeared regularly at appropriate locations to act out eighteenth-century scenes. Among the characters portrayed were slaves and free blacks. By 1980 a group of black actors was developing a living history program specifically focused on black history. As reported in the museum's in-house newspaper, "A special part of the Living History program focuses on black history and the joys and despairs of daily black life in the 18th century" (Colonial Williamsburg Foundation 1980:4). There were also "special programs," more formally staged than character acting. For example, "I Am Many, We Are One" used acting, music, narration, and slides to depict "the history and diversity of Afro-American culture." Its theme was summarized by one of the actors in these terms: "Black culture is a diverse culture originating from numerous experiences [and individuals]. . . . Together, however, they are one people" (Colonial Williamsburg Foundation 1980:4).

In 1981, the museum put into place "the other half" tour (Colonial Williamsburg Foundation 1981a), which is still offered as of this writing. When I took the tour during the course of field research in 1987, it cost $5.00, an additional charge beyond the cost of admission to the museum (such charges are not unusual for what are considered special programs). This tour did not use living history techniques. Our group of ten visitors was greeted by the tour guide, a young black woman, who led us to one of the museum's elegant gardens. There we sat and listened to the first part of the presentation. Our guide explained that "slavery was a very complex institution." She described the indigenous slavery of West Africa which Europeans "plugged into" to create the African slave trade to the Americas. She spoke of African cultures and their interactions with Europeans. Then, marshalling us on to the second part of the tour, she noted "I always like to end up by saying that there were 55 recorded mutinies [on slave ships]."

The second part of the tour was conducted in the gardens and outhouses of the Wythe House, a gentry residence. Here our guide described aspects of the daily life of slaves, speaking of their knowledge, skills, and resourcefulness. Those qualities, we were told, made slaves extremely valuable to their masters, and that value gave slaves at least an informal bargaining power. "The slave would use anything he could to his advantage, believe me," our guide explained. She went on to discuss the living quarters and duties of "house slaves," comparing the relative luxuriousness of their situation to that of the "field-hand slaves." House slaves, we were told, "probably" had a healthier diet than their masters, who ate too many meats and sweets. Then, pointing to a broken chair in one of the slave quarters, she remarked, "I have problems with that chair," suggesting that its owner would have had it repaired.

A final segment of "The Other Half" tour focused on literacy, the buying of freedom, and Afro-American music, spirituality, and religion. At the end of the tour, visitors were handed eighteenth-century Afro-American musical instruments. Our guide taught each visitor how to use the instrument he or she had been given, as well as a particular rhythmic pattern. She then orchestrated the group in a collective performance of Afro-American music. This participatory finale has been part of the tour from the beginning. A photograph in the December 1981 issue of the museum's in-house newspaper shows the Board of Trustees, instruments in hand, "enjoying participating in 'The Other Half' tour" (Colonial Williamsburg Foundation 1981b).

One of the difficulties in presenting "slave culture" in a museum setting is the lack of surviving material culture and appropriate documentation of it. The museum has recently intensified its archeological research of slave quarters. The fruits of this effort are found at Carter's Grove, a plantation several miles from town which is now an important part of Colonial Williamsburg. Though I do not have space to discuss the reconstructed slave quarters of Carter's Grove, it is worth noting that such reconstructions were recently rejected at nearby Monticello, Thomas Jefferson's home in Charlottesville, Virginia. Monticello administrators decided that paucity of documentation made it impossible to reconstruct "authentic" slave quarters. Anthropologists associated with Monticello have questioned whether authenticity was the relevant issue in that decision, pointing out that reconstruction of the elaborately presented domestic space of Monticello has relied on inferential evidence.[2] Clearly, the decision to maintain Monticello as a private home, rather than the domestic village that historical and archaeological research indicates it to have been, involves considerations beyond those related to "authenticity." That Colonial Williamsburg has chosen to reconstruct slave quarters, despite problems of authentification, indicates a different politics of interpretation from that recently played out at Monticello.

The dynamics of interactions between Colonial Williamsburg "slaves" and audiences (predominantly but not exclusively white) are complex and can only be suggested here. The interpreter who pioneered the role-playing of slaves told me that when he started, he used uninterrupted "first person" (this means that he did not "break frame" to explain himself or his role to the audience). However, he soon found first-person to be "too intense" both for audiences and for actors. Thus he began to alternate between first- and third-person. This allowed him to explain the slave role to the audience, thereby assuaging their anxiety. At the same time, distancing himself from his slave role helped him to cope with his own shame. This technique is standard today.

As for audiences, when they are told during tours of particular buildings that they will now meet a slave, they become tense. Black interpreters meet these audiences boldly, teasing them about their shyness and their strange (to eighteenth-century eyes) clothing. In both first- and third-person, slaves are depicted as powerful, resourceful, clever people whose worth to their masters not only gives them some measure of protection from arbitrary cruelties, but some degree of political or economic power. Audiences seem relieved to find dynamic slaves played by skilled actors. "You were wonderful," sighed one woman as she thanked a historical interpreter after the performance.

For an analysis of ethnic ideology, what is crucial about the depiction of "The Other Half" at Colonial Williamsburg is the insistence that slaves "have a culture." The cruelties and injustices of slavery are suggested, but interpretive narratives insist upon the creative response Afro-Americans made to them. Such responses are shown to have embodied themselves in "a culture" that allowed slaves "to lead lives worth living even . . . under cultural domination" (Colonial Williamsburg Foundation 1985:5). The museum displays this culture with artifacts and archeological exhibits. But, given the paucity of remains, it is the living history program—bringing slaves to life as "resourceful" characters readily admirable to twentieth-century Americans—that brings home the message of a distinctive cultural identity.

I would suggest that the decision to depict an individuated "slave culture" is based on the presuppositions of possessive individualism, as sketched above, rather than on strict considerations of authenticity. This is so despite the explicit ideology of those responsible for black history at Colonial Williamsburg. "We discover the truth and present it to the public," explained one of the first black character interpreters (Colonial Williamsburg Foundation 1980). Such statements are echoed by most museum historians, who, whatever their understanding of the interpretive element in historical writing and research, subscribe to a positivist historiography. Thus they seek "accuracy" and consistently underestimate, in my opinion, the power of present-day concerns to permeate interpretations of the past. In the present case, to depict the lives of Afro-Americans as representative of one individuated culture—"I Am Many, We Are One"—creates a sense of cultural unity and identity that might well be disputed from a perspective other than that of possessive individualism. Indeed, the diversity of Afro-American cultural traditions is also celebrated in the slave history of Colonial Williamsburg. However, as I have argued elsewhere (Handler 1988:6, 175–181), in ideologies of ethnic identity, homogeneity and unity ultimately override internal diversity. "Afro-American culture" is presented to the public as an unproblematic entity.

Whether this interpretive outlook sins against "accuracy" is of less concern to me than its political import. As I suggested above, individuated cultures, each possessed of their "property" (in the form of museum props), become equivalent. Thus the Colonial Williamsburg master plan for the "Becoming Americans" theme speaks of the contributions of various ethnic groups (described as "separate yet interdependent societies") to the American whole (Colonial Williamsburg Foundation 1985:5). Though domination and injustices are discussed, there is little analysis of the social interactions of human beings (of various "ethnic" backgrounds) in terms of exploitation and power relations. Indeed, to portray domination it might be better *not* to imagine the past in terms of equivalent collective individuals participating, however unequally, in a common task of nation-building. Rather, museums should present explicit analysis of the *system* of racism and colonial exploitation. In other words, the social unit to be made salient by museum interpretation might be the racist social system, rather than ethnic cultures within it. Or, as Terrence Epperson puts it in a useful critique of black history at Colonial Williamsburg, "over-emphasizing the autonomy of slave culture runs the risk of mystifying relations of power" (Epperson 1988:5).[3]

The presentation of the Afro-American culture of "the other half" at Colonial Williamsburg gratifies both black and white museum professionals and audiences. The possessive-individualistic assumptions of the program speak to our present-day desires. Black activists can proudly claim their cultural heritage, and whites sympathetic to their cause can join in the celebration of that heritage. But, as Epperson reminds us, "ours is still an essentially racist society" (1988:2). To focus on the "contributions" of an individuated Afro-American culture makes it too easy to forget not only the racism of colonial society, but the racism of our own society. Exploitation and racism are banished to the past, when slavery existed, and even the horrors of slavery are minimized by the representation of resourceful slaves and the slaves' cultural resources. The suggested shift in museum focus is not to denigrate or overlook the remarkable histories of Afro-Americans. Instead, I would argue that to deconstruct the possessive-individualistic assumptions of ethnicity in the museum is a first step toward an understanding of how racism continues to victimize modern Americans. Museums must continue to experiment with the portrayal of ethnic inequality as it existed in the past and persists in the present.

Notes

[1]For a historical and descriptive account of the living history "movement," written by one of its leading advocates, see Anderson (1984). For a critique of the epistemology of living history, see Handler (1987).

[2]I owe these observations to Jeffrey Hantman and Eric Gable of the Department of Anthropology, University of Virginia. For a pioneering programmatic statement of the possibilities for an archeology of slavery in North America, see Deetz (1977:138–154).

[3]Epperson's paper (1988), as well as discussions with him, have been particularly useful to me in formulating the arguments of the final paragraphs.

References Cited

Alexander, Edward
1979 Museums in Motion. Nashville: American Association for State and Local History.

Anderson, Jay
1984 Time Machines: The World of Living History. Nashville: American Association for State and Local History.

Colonial Williamsburg Foundation
1952 Central Employment Office to Open in Broadened Colonial Williamsburg Personnel Program. Colonial Williamsburg News 5(8):1, 4.
1980 Combined Talents Create Scenes of Black History. Colonial Williamsburg News 33(8):4–5.
1981a Tour Shows "The Other Half." Colonial Williamsburg News 34(8):3.
1981b Board Tours Behind-the-Scenes. Colonial Williamsburg News 34(12):3.
1985 Teaching History at Colonial Williamsburg. Williamsburg: Colonial Williamsburg Foundation.

Deetz, James
1977 In Small Things Forgotten: The Archeology of Early American Life. Garden City, NY: Anchor Books.

Dumont, Louis
1970 Religion, Politics, and Society in the Individualistic Universe. Proceedings of the Royal Anthropological Institute of Great Britain and Ireland, pp. 31–41.

Epperson, Terrence
1988 Discussion of "The Other Half." Paper presented at the annual meeting of the American Society for Ethnohistory, Williamsburg, VA, November 12.
Evans-Pritchard, E. E.
1937 Witchcraft, Oracles and Magic Among the Azande. Oxford: Oxford University Press.
Fraser, Gertrude, and Reginald Butler
1986 The Unmaking of Afro-American History *In* Presenting the Past. S. P Benson, et al., eds. Philadelphia: Temple University Press.
Goodwin, W. A. R.
1937 The Restoration of Colonial Williamsburg. National Geographic 71(4):402–443.
Handler, Richard
1985 On Having a Culture: Nationalism and the Preservation of Quebec's *Patrimoine*. History of Anthropology 3:192–217
1987 Overpowered by Realism: Living History and the Simulation of the Past. Journal of American Folklore 100:337–341.
1988 Nationalism and the Politics of Culture in Quebec. Madison: University of Wisconsin Press.
Macpherson, C. B.
1962 The Political Theory of Possessive Individualism: Hobbes to Locke. Oxford: Oxford University Press.
Wagner, Roy
1975 The Invention of Culture. Englewood Cliffs, NJ: Prentice-Hall.

Measuring Ethnicity and Its Political Consequences in a Southern Appalachian High School

Susan E. Keefe, Gregory G. Reck, and Una Mae Lange Reck

This paper analyzes survey data from a larger research project focusing on education in a county in western North Carolina. This region of Appalachia, dominated by the tourism and recreation industry, has experienced considerable in-migration in the last two decades, and over 20% of the county's population is made up of recent non-Appalachian inmigrants (Keefe 1988). Economic differences between the native Appalachians and the better-off non-Appalachian newcomers are readily apparent. Perceptions of difference are more likely to be stated in ethnic terms, however, using distinctions like local/outsider or mountain people/ flatlander to label the two groups.

Political differences between the two groups have emerged, particularly over land use issues and legalization of the more widespread sale of alcohol, and sensitivity over group membership has increased over the years and has become acute in the county's only high school, the single local institution in which all social segments of the county must interact on a regular basis. Our interest was in the application of the concept of ethnicity as a way of better understanding the inequitable access to education of Appalachian natives in the county, who have much lower levels of academic achievement and higher rates of dropping out as compared to non-Appalachians.

We describe the development of a quantitative means of distinguishing Appalachians from non-Appalachians and the significance of this technique for the evaluation of ethnicity and its associated impact on students. The emotionally charged controversy at the research site caused by our application of the concept of ethnicity and by our use of survey methods for its measurement is also discussed. Our experience also makes it abundantly clear that applied anthropologists must come to appreciate the practical implications of emic perceptions of ethnicity and learn to maneuver within these perceptions if they are to intervene effectively in policy making.

In 1983, we began this research project to determine the extent to which ethnicity, especially as distinct from socioeconomic class and rural/ urban residence, contributes to the divergence in educational attainment between mountain people and newcomers in Appalachia. A model of ethnicity was developed to include three general dimensions: structural, cultural, and symbolic (Keefe, Reck, and Reck 1983). Structural ethnicity refers to the boundedness and opposition of groups within the larger society. Cultural ethnicity is based on a distinctive pattern of traits shared by members of a group. Lastly, symbolic ethnicity puts emphasis on ethnic identification and perceived cultural differences. These are conceived of as distinctive though interrelated dimensions of ethnicity in general. According to this definition, then, ethnicity refers to the distinctiveness of two or more groups which are in contact yet set apart in structural, cultural, and symbolic ways.

Our research involved the collection of ethnographic, archival, and survey data. The focus for research was the county's consolidated high school, but considerable effort was made to understand the community context. Toward the end of the data collection phase of the research, a survey was developed to measure several aspects for each of the three dimensions of ethnicity. Four aspects of structural ethnicity were tapped, including the presence and perception of group boundaries, ethnic political differences, and group prejudice and discrimination. Six aspects of cultural ethnicity were examined involving regional dialect, regional foods, musical preferences, religion and church affiliation, gender roles, and kinship patterns. Finally, symbolic ethnicity covered the three aspects of ethnic identification, ethnic pride, and the perception of and attachment to cultural differences.

The survey was administered by high school teachers, with the county school superintendent's and the principal's permission, to all students present during regular class time on a single day in the spring of 1985. The 146 questions took approximately 30 minutes to complete. Students were provided with machine-ready answer forms to facilitate computerization of the data. A total of 795 usable answer sheets was returned, forming the final student sample.

The Construction of Empirical Dimensions

In an initial analysis of the survey results, the responses of Appalachian students (identified by asking for the birthplace of the student and his or her mother and father) were significantly different from non-Appalachian students on 93% of the items designed to measure structural, cultural, and symbolic ethnicity (Keefe, Reck, and Reck 1985). Furthermore, students of mixed descent (that is, one or two of the three family members—student, student's mother, and student's father—were born in Appalachia while the other family member(s) were born outside the region) tended to have a third pattern of response that fell between the patterns for Appalachians and non-Appalachians, indicating the more or less consistent process of cultural blending one might expect in such group contact situations.

Subsequently, the survey data were factor analyzed to determine the extent of internal consistency in the hypothesized aspects and dimensions of ethnicity.[1] Each of the 94 items appropriate for factor analysis was scaled in the direction of Appalachian ethnicity so that a high score reflected greater structural, cultural, and symbolic "Appalachianness" as distinct from mainstream American ethnicity. First-order factor analysis produced a total of 15 factors using 71 variables distributed as hypothesized over the three dimensions.

Second-order factor analysis was then carried out using factor-based scales created by summing the variables contributing to each of the first-order factors. This analysis produced five second-order factors. Finally, these second-order factors were converted to factor-based scales and submitted to factor analysis, and two independent factors were obtained. The items and sub-factors contributing to these final third-order factors, labelled "Ethnicity" and "Perception of Roles and Statuses," are summarized in the appendix.

The emergence of the Ethnicity Factor supports our hypothesis that structural, cultural, and symbolic dimensions contribute theoretically to ethnicity. These are measured by the dimensions of Ethnic Association, Symbolic Attachment, and Cultural Affiliation. Regression confirms that Appalachian group membership (as defined by student's and parents' birthplace) explains 47% of the variance in this factor, while rural residence (as defined in this case by county elementary school attended), male sex, and father's education explain an additional 5% of the variance.

The emergence of the second factor, which we call Perception of Roles and Statuses, is more difficult to explain. Examination of alternative analyses indicates that if the aspect of Perception of Prejudice and Discrimination were more robust and had more variables contributing to its formulation, it would form a factor separate from the Perception of Gender Roles. As presently formulated, this factor appears to encompass the perception of distinctive roles and statuses for males and females as well as for ethnic groups. Very little of the variance can be accounted for in regression analysis by any of the independent variables we measured; in particular, ethnic group membership is not significantly correlated with this second factor.

In summary, using the example of Southern Appalachians, we can demonstrate the empirical measurement of three dimensions of ethnicity, all of which are distinctive yet interrelated constructs. As such, the analysis reaffirms the need to investigate ethnicity using a multidimensional approach, rather than rely on reductionist approaches which fail to fully comprehend the shifting nature of ethnicity. Furthermore, the factors isolated in the analysis of data on Appalachians are similar in content to those found in a study among Chicanos (Keefe and Padilla 1987), adding reliability to our theoretical model based on structural, cultural, and symbolic dimensions of ethnicity. The factors of Appalachian ethnicity correlate highly with the self-evaluations of academic success asked for on the survey, including items on high school grade average, tracking level of high school courses, and the intention to go on to college. While students' socioeconomic status and rural/urban residence are also (and sometimes more highly) correlated with these indicators of academic success, the data demonstrate that ethnicity must be taken into consideration as an independent factor in any policy changes made to improve education in Appalachia. In other words, educational reform should by all means include culturally based intervention such as increasing the use of regional literature in the classroom, selecting textbooks that treat the region in a positive rather than stereotypical manner, and incorporating classroom and counseling techniques to enhance Appalachian students' ethnic pride.

Applied Consequences

From the beginning, we felt that our research would be of interest to teachers, administrators, and policy makers as well as academicians. It was our intent to report on the results of our research to the local school system that was the object of study, and regional agencies interested in the improvement of Appalachian schools. We realized in doing preliminary fieldwork that the topics which interested us were of a sensitive nature and that special effort was needed to ensure a successful project. Prior to the ethnicity survey, our progress seemed to indicate that we had succeeded in this regard. We took care to include the school superintendent in our plans for research, and he willingly wrote a letter in support of our grant proposal. We were received graciously by students, parents, teachers, and school administrators alike in the course of observation and interviewing.

We administered without problems a student participation survey in the high school during the initial phase of the research project. The ethnicity survey was to be the final component of the data collection process (Reck, Keefe, and Reck 1986). The survey, entitled simply "Attitude Survey," was made up of questions asked without problem during a number of the personal interviews conducted over the previous year. The survey was pre-tested and was submitted for approval to both the school system superintendent and the high school principal, who seemed concerned primarily that the survey not interfere with instructional time. The principal himself offered to take responsibility for its administration. Thus, despite the sensitivity of some of the questions, we felt relatively secure that no problems would arise.

We were wrong. Many of the students and teachers were outraged at some of the questions on the survey, feeling they were prejudiced. A number refused to complete the survey, and about 40 students handed in written comments in response to the survey. The following will serve as examples:

> "Are you a hillbilly? I sure ain't! I'm from Florida—and proud of it!"

> "I think you are making all of us look like hillbillies. . . I also think you are making people from Florida is better than the ones who live in the mountains."

"Sure we're different. But we are still human beings. Just because we talk a little different doesn't mean we act different. I would rather live in the mountains than anywhere else any day."

"I am a hillbilly and proud of it. But I dress and act just as good as a newcomer. I am a farmer too."

"I'm from Gary, Indiana, and I'm not prejudiced. Whoever made this survey obviously is."

Some of the students took copies of the survey home to be read by parents, friends and neighbors. What had begun as a school event soon became a focus for the entire community, and we felt the effects in our private as well as professional lives. For many days, we faced jokes, snide comments, and cold shoulders from neighbors, co-workers, and informants. Over the next several weeks, there were news stories on the local radio station and in the local newspaper, letters to the editor from critics and supporters, and meetings with the county school board and the faculty of the high school. We wrote a letter to be distributed to all students at the high school which explained more fully the purpose of our research and apologized for any misunderstandings the survey produced. We were in doubt as to whether we still might contribute in a positive way to the local schools.

While a full analysis of this experience cannot be attempted here, some discussion of the concept of ethnicity as it is understood by Americans and as it is experienced in American schools is relevant. Equality and individualism are core American values whose virtues are impressed upon students during their years of formal education (Mead 1965; Warner 1953). For anthropologists, trained to apply cultural relativism in some respect, ethnic differences are appreciated as interesting variations on what it is to be human and are not the object of value judgements. For Americans in general, on the other hand, ethnic differences are equated with ethnic stratification—in truth, the reality of their social world. In fact, the term "ethnicity" is perceived as implying the judgment that some groups are "better" than others and, therefore, the act of bringing greater attention to differences may be interpreted as reinforcing that inequality. In this sense, by simply asking about differences, we were perceived as prejudiced by those reading the survey. Finally, the study of ethnicity implies that group membership determines individual opportunities, and while this may be considered a truism to social scientists, it contrasts sharply with the American ideals of independence and individualism. This explains many of the students' objections to lumping people into categories and their insistence that "people are individuals." At the same time, some students felt that they might be wrongly lumped into a lower status group—a special concern of middle-class native Appalachian students who use their socioeconomic status to negotiate out of the forced negative identity reserved for local people in general.

The implication is that despite the publicly admired values of individualism and equality, students and non-students are also very much aware of the social divisions in the community. In fact, it is in the single county high school, a microcosm of the larger community, where these divisions appear most sharply—a point our informants consistently confirmed in private interviews. Yet, these divisions which threaten the social fabric are often denied in the formal public sphere and, due to the absence of obvious cultural or racial markers, that denial generally goes uncontested. The superintendent, for example, in endorsing our grant proposal entitled "Ethnicity and Education in Southern Appalachia" questioned our use of the term *ethnicity* because "everyone here is the same" (i.e., white Anglo Americans). In the public context of the classroom where students taking our survey could look up and most likely see Appalachian and non-Appalachian, middle and lower class, and rural and urban students, respondents were asked to make something which was in many ways culturally implicit and covert into something explicit and overt. As one teacher commented later, "I guess it [the survey] was too threatening."

The experience with the survey simultaneously increased our understanding of the educational context and limited our ability to have a direct impact upon it. Impressed with the community's perception of the term "ethnicity," we omitted reference to it and our interest in ethnic theory from the preliminary report presented over a year later to the local school system, speaking instead of "cultural differences" and "sociocultural groups." The new superintendent (a perceptive administrator and native of the county who replaced the superintendent with whom we originally had worked) received the report enthusiastically while proceeding with caution in sharing it with others. At a subsequently arranged group meeting with all of the county school principals, our report and the incorporated suggestions for the schools produced only cursory discussion. We offered assistance in several ways (teacher workshops, curriculum development, etc.) at various times during our meetings with the superintendent and school administrators, but we received little encouragement.

After several months had passed, we received a brief letter from the superintendent thanking us for the report while declining further assistance. The letter read in part:

> While we have identified several areas that need our attention, we have decided to not make open issues of any. We have basically decided that this is the proper position for us because of potential negative reaction that could be generated and because it might bring out old feelings that are best left undisturbed.

Despite our personal disappointment with this decision, we are confident that our research and the report (which was also eventually distributed by the superintendent to the elected members of the county school board) have had some impact on policy making in the schools.

For example, whereas prior personnel hiring practices for the elementary schools had given preference in the name of "cost effectiveness" to the largest school, which was also located in the non-Appalachian dominated urban center, the superintendent subsequently began to recommend decentralization of hiring to ensure coverage at the Appalachian-native dominated rural schools. The school board, which had resisted the idea of a second rural-situated county high school despite strong backing by Appalachian residents, chose to seek support for such a high school the following year with a bond issue. While the bond failed to win approval by county voters, the board moved to use monies already at their disposal to rebuild an elementary (K-8th grade) school in a rural Appalachian dominated part of the county rather than opt for a new educational plan incorporating centralized middle schools—a plan favored more by non-Appalachian urban residents. In these and other decisions we see evidence of a shift in the county's educational policy making, giving, in the words of the superintendent, "equal treatment" to all students.

Conclusion

People of the southern mountains are an interesting group with which to test theories of ethnicity because they constitute a borderline case, considered by some researchers to be equivalent to a distinctive ethnic group and by other researchers to be simply one more segment of the larger white Protestant mainstream American population. For the most part, this disagreement revolves around an evaluation of the distinctiveness of Appalachian cultural traits and values (see, for example, Billings 1974; Fisher 1978, versus Jones 1978; Pearsall 1966). Researchers are much more likely to agree that mountaineers are perceived as different by others (as, for example, in the hillbilly stereotype) and that they have been exploited by the larger society (Batteau 1980; Gaventa 1980; Lewis, Johnson, and Askins 1978).

One might assume, therefore, that even if cultural ethnicity did not emerge as significant in an empirical study, symbolic and structural Appalachian ethnicity would still be apparent. It is hard to imagine, however, a situation in which symbolic and structural differences alone would set ethnic groups apart, unsupported by any observable differences in cultural traits. Structural separation of groups would create a situation in which cultural distinctiveness could be maintained or would develop over time if it were not already present, and, if cultural differences did not exist in the past, one would expect them to be created in order to support the idea of symbolic difference (Keefe 1986). In sum, while the relative importance of the three dimensions of ethnicity might vary in the application to Appalachians, one might expect all of them to contribute in the final analysis to Appalachian ethnicity.

We have described here a multidimensional model of ethnicity and confirmed with quantitative data the ethnic nature of the white native population of southern Appalachia. It is supported by our more qualitative data which also indicates that, while cultural differences do distinguish mountain people from newcomers, structural and symbolic ethnicity are more significant than cultural ethnicity in the construction of what it means to be Appalachian. Thus, it helps to make sense of the difficulty people (both Appalachian and non-Appalachian) have in dealing with the concept of "mountain people": they "know" they exist but they cannot articulate many distinctive cultural traits beyond recalling stereotypes.

In the educational context, this often results in school administrators and teachers as well as parents and students (1) blaming the "distinctive" culture of mountain kids for their educational failure and simultaneously (2) denying that mountain kids are culturally different and might have different educational needs or might be discriminated against as a group in the school system. As a result, native Appalachian students on the whole have low self-esteem, become ambivalent about their cultural heritage, experience an inadequate education, and often blame themselves individually for their lack of educational success rather than conclude that Appalachians as a group are treated unequally.

Clearly, the application of ethnic theory to the study of educational systems in Appalachia can enhance our understanding of the native Appalachian experience. In the specific case described in this chapter, it was the use of a model of ethnicity which helped to clarify the educational context for the anthropologists and the diversity of the student population for the school policymakers and to better ensure equal access to educational resources by all county residents.

Notes

Acknowledgments. Appreciation is extended to NSF for funding the research on which this paper is based (Grant No. BNS-8218234). Keefe would also like to acknowledge a grant from Graduate Studies and Research, and funding from the Department of Anthropology, Appalachian State University, which supported the quantitative analysis of the ethnic attitudes survey data. The statistical analysis was completed with the help of Rose Coley and Deanna Bowman.

[1]A complete description of the factor analysis performed can be found in Keefe, Reck, and Reck (1987). The procedure followed was that of principal factoring with iterations and a Varimax rotation method to extract factors.

References Cited

Batteau, Allen
1980 Appalachia and the Concept of Culture: A Theory of Shared Misunderstandings. Appalachian Journal 7(1–2):9–31

Billings, Dwight
1974 Culture and Poverty in Appalachia: A Theoretical Discussion and Empirical Analysis. Social Forces 53:315–323.

Fisher, Stephen L.
1978 Victim-blaming in Appalachia: Cultural Theories and the Southern Mountaineer. *In* Appalachia: Social Context Past and Present. Bruce Ergood and Bruce Kuhre, eds. Dubuque, IA: Kendall/Hunt.

Gaventa, John
1980 Power and Powerlessness: Quiescence and Rebellion in an Appalachian Valley Urbana: University of Illinois Press.

Jones, Loyal
1978 Appalachian Values. *In* Appalachia: Social Context Past and Present. Bruce Ergood and Bruce Kuhre, eds. Dubuque, IA: Kendall/Hunt.
Keefe, Susan Emley
1986 Southern Appalachia: Analytical Models, Social Services, and Native Support Systems. American Journal of Community Psychology 14:479–498.
1988 An Exploratory Study of Mental Health Service Utilization Comparing Appalachian Natives and Non-Appalachian Immigrants. *In* Appalachian Mental Health. Susan Emley Keefe, ed. Lexington: University Press of Kentucky
Keefe, Susan E. and Amado M. Padilla
1987 Chicano Ethnicity. Albuquerque: University of New Mexico Press.
Keefe, Susan E., Gregory G. Reck, and Una Mae Reck
1985 Ethnicity and Education in Southern Appalachia: Do Mountaineers Fit the Ethnic Minority Model? Paper presented at the annual meeting of the American Anthropological Association, Washington, D.C., December 5.
1987 Dimensions of Ethnicity: What it Means to be Native Appalachian in a Southern Mountain High School. Paper presented at the annual meeting of the American Anthropological Association, Chicago, November 21.
Keefe, Susan E., Una Mae L. Reck, and Gregory G. Reck
1983 Ethnicity and Education in Southern Appalachia: A Review. Ethnic Groups 5:199–226.
Lewis, Helen, Linda Johnson, and Donald Askins, eds.
1978 Colonialism in Modern America: The Appalachian Case. Boone, NC: Appalachian Consortium Press.
Mead, Margaret
1965 And Keep Your Powder Dry. New York: William Morrow.
Pearsall, Marion
1966 Communicating with the Educationally Deprived. Mountain Life & Work 42(1):8–11.
Reck, Gregory G., Susan E. Keefe, and Una Mae L. Reck
1986 Method as Data: Serendipity in an Appalachian Research Project. Paper presented at the annual meeting of the Southern Anthropological Society, Wrightsville Beach, NC, April 24.
Warner, W. Lloyd
1953 American Life: Dream and Reality Chicago: University of Chicago Press.

Appendix

Survey Items and Subfactors Producing Third-Order Factors of Ethnicity and Perception of Roles and Statuses

I. Ethnicity Factor
   A. Ethnic Association Subfactor
      1. Intraethnic Social Networks
         a. School friends speak like mountain people
         b. Neighborhood friends speak like mountain people
      2. Preference for Ethnic Associates
         a. Prefers natives in clubs
         b. Prefers natives at parties
         c. Does not prefer newcomers in clubs
         d. Prefers natives as neighbors
         e. Does not prefer newcomers as neighbors
         f. Prefers marriage to native
         g. Does not prefer newcomers at parties
         h. Does not prefer marriage to non-Appalachians
   B. Symbolic Attachment Subfactor
      1. Appalachian Ethnic Pride
         a. Believes mountain people share
         b. Believes mountain people are friendly
         c. Believes mountain people are hardworking
         d. Believes mountain people are polite
         e. Believes mountain people are not lazy
         f. Believes mountain people have dependable kin
         g. Believes mountain people are not greedy
      2. Appalachian Ethnic Identity
         a. Identifies as "Mountaineer"
         b. Identifies as "Mountain people"
         c. Identifies as "Appalachian"
         d. Identifies as "Native"
         e. Local county identity
         f. Identifies as "Local"
         g. Identifies as "Country people"
         h. Identifies as "Highlander"
         i. Identifies as "Hillbilly"
      3. Lack non-Appalachian Ethnic Pride
         a. Believes newcomers are not friendly
         b. Believes newcomers do not share
         c. Believes newcomers are impolite
         d. Believes newcomers are not hardworking
         e. Believes newcomers do not have dependable kin
      4. Lack non-Appalachian Ethnic Identity
         a. Does not identify as "Newcomer"

b. Does not identify as "Outsider"
c. Does not identify as "Yankee"
5. Attachment to Mountains
a. Prefers never to move out of mountains
b. Wants to own land in mountains
c. Feels strongly attached to mountains
C. Cultural Affiliation Subfactor
1. Appalachian Dialect
a. Speaks differently from non-Appalachians
b. Speaks like mountain people
c. Understands mountain people
d. Misunderstands non-Appalachians
2. Appalachian Diet
a. Often eats cornbread
b. Often eats pinto beans
c. Often eats cabbage
d. Often eats biscuits
3. Local Kin Network
a. Local kin give aid
b. Gives local kin aid
c. Many kin visited monthly
d. Many kin visited weekly
e. High number of local kin
4. Religiousness
a. Goes to church often
b. Attends church
c. Reads the Bible often
5. Family Reunions
a. Attended reunion recently
b. Family has reunions often

II. Perception of Roles and Statuses Factor
A. Perception of Prejudice and Discrimination Subfactor
1. Believes mountain people dislike newcomers
2. Believes newcomers dislike mountain people
3. Believes mountain people are discriminated against
4. Believes newcomers are discriminated against
B. Perception of Gender Roles Subfactor
1. Female Gender Roles
a. Believes inappropriate for women to chop wood
b. Believes inappropriate for women to plow fields
c. Believes inappropriate for women to harvest tobacco
d. Believes inappropriate for women to hunt
e. Believes inappropriate for women to do car repair
f. Believes inappropriate for women to fish
2. Male Gender Role

a. Believes inappropriate for men to vacuum
b. Believes inappropriate for men to wash dishes
c. Believes inappropriate for men to clean bathroom
d. Believes inappropriate for men to babysit
e. Believes inappropriate for men to cook
f. Believes inappropriate for men to can food
g. Believes inappropriate for men to sew

Source: Authors' Ethnic Attitudes Survey of high school students.

Cultural Relevance in the Delivery of Human Services

M. Jean Gilbert

For the past ten years I have been involved in applied anthropological research in California. Most of my work has compared Mexican Americans and Anglo Americans or has focused specifically on Mexican Americans; and I have ranged rather widely in subject area, dealing with educational issues, family services, maternal and child health, and alcohol use and abuse. Because I have been eager to see my research data applied in service delivery, I have spent considerable time training, consulting with, and rendering technical assistance to planners and providers of public services. It is in these contexts that I frequently hear the term "culturally relevant services" used.

The notion of cultural relevancy is based on the understanding that ethnic groups are set apart from each other by unique world views, systems of values, interactive roles, behavioral styles, and, often, languages; in sum, each has its unique culture. What is real and relevant to members of one ethnic group may not have the same salience and value in another. In addition, in a pluralistic society, ethnic groups are frequently distinguished from each other by differential access to social, political and economic power. And yet, what occurs all too frequently is that the administrators who allocate funds, create policy, and plan and design human services do so only with the characteristics, norms, and behaviors of the majority group in mind. Because these programs lack meaning to members of ethnic minority groups whose cultural orientation is based on different values and interpretations of reality, the helping services fail to attract, retain, or aid persons in these ethnic groups. These circumstances have both practical and ethical implications.

On a practical level, there is tremendous financial loss of scarce resources when programs fail or inadequately respond to the needs of people they are intended to help. Human problems that do not get solved tend to compound, become entrenched, and ultimately require costlier solutions. On an ethical level, our commitment to a democratic society requires that we provide equal access to the benefits provided by that society, regardless of religion, gender, color, race, age, or ethnicity. Consistency requires that our public institutions reflect that recognition of human variation. These ideas are hardly new, but they bear repeating because they provide an important context for the issue of cultural relevancy as it applies to public services.

Accessibility is based on relevance. In order to access services effectively, people must know that they exist and understand what they are for and how they work. They must perceive a relationship between the services offered and the life problems they are experiencing. Since both the delivery and acceptance of services are, at base, volitional acts, they must arise out of providers' and clients' mutual trust and understanding of the actions to be taken. There must also be a consonance of purpose between provider and client in order for each to take and sustain action. These necessary mutualities do not exist (and their absence limits accessibility for ethnic minority clients) when the provider fails, through ignorance or ethnocentrism, to recognize and be sensitive to the world view and social ecology of the client. Therefore, achieving cultural relevance and expanding access to human services requires that service planners and providers acquire knowledge about ethnic groups targeted for service and use this knowledge in the planning and design of programs.

Critical problems concerning the cultural relevance of services presently exist in the United States, and anthropologists are better equipped than most to appreciate their seriousness and devise strategies toward their resolution. The ethnic populations immigrating to the United States in the last fifteen years are highly varied and tend to be nonwestern in contrast to the vast majority of immigrants in earlier waves of immigration. Their cultures differ more from the mainstream than was true for earlier immigrant groups. Many also come from areas of the world that are less industrialized than the United States, and this results in a modern/traditional cultural gap. And some have entered our borders demoralized by war and political persecution, clinging tenaciously to the security provided by their traditional cultural order and fearful of the inevitable erosion of that order in their new and often precarious circumstances.

The concern in a pluralistic and democratic society for "culturally sensitive," "culturally appropriate" or "culturally relevant" services is therefore a legitimate and serious one and deserves more careful consideration than it is often given—both by those who advocate such services and those whose responsibility it is to provide them. These terms are often used, however, to mean little else than that more persons of a certain ethnicity or more speakers of a particular language should be employed in a given service arena. Participation by members of a given ethnic group in the planning and provision of services for that group is certainly one very important component of making services accessible to group members. So is rendering services in the language of the target group, but cultural relevance as a concept cannot be reduced to these two elements.

Cultural relevance should have an impact on public services at all levels of the service-providing structure. It is vitally important for the clinician, counselor, social worker, or other provider of direct services to be culturally sensitive in face-to-face interaction with clients. This need for cultural relevance at interface is well accepted in theory if not in practice. Less well perceived, however, is the need to incorporate the concept in needs assessments, planning and prioritizing, training, personnel management, and resource allocation.

The examples in this article are drawn from my experience and highlight specific kinds of information needed to achieve cultural relevance at different levels in the service-providing structure. I will argue that greater concreteness and situational specificity are needed to create culturally relevant interventions and helping strategies in direct service contexts. Finally, I will offer a few recommendations for applied anthropologists who wish to have their ethnographic research used to promote greater cultural relevance in the provision of human services.

Toward Culturally Relevant Planning and Funding

For culturally relevant decision making in the overall planning and funding of services, it is critical that baseline data defining demographic differences and similarities between the targeted ethnic population and the larger population be obtained. Whether planning is being done by a state or local agency, it is important that planners know the unique characteristics of an ethnic population, such as population size and mean age, education, income, and family size. For example, in California it would be important to know that the Mexican American population is much younger than the general U.S. population, with a mean age of 23 compared to 33 in the general population.

Why is this important? Because knowing it casts light on data relating to service utilization and client characteristics. For instance, Mexican American males are slightly overrepresented in the alcohol treatment population in terms of population parity. However, considering that client statistics are drawn from an over-eighteen year old population and that this population is proportionately much smaller within the Mexican American ethnic group, one can see that over-representation of Mexican American males in alcohol treatment takes on more significance. Men in this ethnic group clearly need and utilize alcohol treatment services, and planners and resource allocators need to know this.

Additionally, for any service area, differences between at-risk levels of the ethnic population and the larger population should be consistently assessed. It is critical, for example, in any health field to have epidemiological and service utilization data broken down by ethnicity to determine whether an ethnic group is more or less at risk for a particular health problem than are persons in the larger population.

The prevalent bureaucratic practice of creating catch-all "ethnic" labels such as "Hispanic," "Native American," or "Asian" is an obstacle to the design of culturally relevant programs. When implemented in data gathering, this unfortunate practice prevents accurate descriptions of ethnic groups by clustering culturally variant groups under a convenient label such as "Hispanic" and then treating this artificially constructed category as an "ethnic" group when survey data are analyzed.

Descriptive national or state survey data aggregated in this way are virtually useless for determining at-risk levels across ethnic groups and thus for accurately allocating funds for regional and local services. For example, on almost any demographic or socioeconomic indicator Mexican Americans and Cuban Americans differ significantly. Their alcohol use patterns also differ as Cubans are much less at risk than Mexican Americans for problems related to alcohol (Caetano 1987). When data from these two groups are aggregated, the result is a "no group" description useless for the purpose of assessing need for services or matching client characteristics with treatment modalities.

Addressing the issue of cultural relevance at the planning and policymaking level, therefore, requires more specificity in the methods and the data used to inform planning. Something as basic as expanding client intake forms to include information on ethnicity and analyzing service utilization by ethnic group is culturally sensitive in the planning context (Giachello 1985). Needs assessments can also be designed to collect more detailed ethnic data, and year-end reports can provide ethnic breakdowns.

Ethnographic data in combination with survey findings can be used by policymakers to determine significant within-group differences in risk status which can result in more focused program planning. If such epidemiological data are not available, it would be a culturally relevant planning decision to allocate funds and devise methods for obtaining them. For instance, say we are given the task of allocating funds for various types of county alcohol-related programs. Research has disclosed that there is a much higher male:female ratio of alcohol problems among Mexican Americans than is the case in the larger population (Gilbert and Cervantes 1987). Therefore, a culturally relevant decision in a locality with a heavy concentration of this group could be to allocate the major portion of treatment funds to male-oriented programs and direct funds for outreach, prevention, and support groups to women and children in alcohol-troubled families. Conversely, if a community alcohol center is located in an area with a high proportion of older, single, acculturated Mexican American women, the only female Mexican American group with a high rate of alcohol problems according to Caetano and Medina-Mora (1986), the culturally relevant decision could be to allocate a sizable proportion of program funds to outreach and casefinding within this subgroup.

The structural characteristics of an ethnic group vis-à-vis the larger population also need to be considered in setting overall program directions that will have long-term impact on the nature of services of a specific kind. For example, the organization of prevention activities in alcoholism services has undergone a rapid and radical change in the last five years. Prevention philosophy has shifted emphasis from educational activities directed toward achieving behavioral changes (largely unsuccessful) in individuals, to an emphasis on altering the ecology of drinking environments with a corresponding focus on the prevention of specific societal problems (i.e., drunk driving, family violence) created by alcohol use. Thus current activities fostered and funded by state and county agencies are geared toward regulating drinking and drinking environments through taxation, licensing and zoning restrictions, tougher enforcement of existing liquor laws, and regulation of media advertising. These efforts, however, largely depend upon the efforts of grassroots community organizations to advocate and create these policies. Funds are therefore being allocated to such local-level advocacy groups under statewide "master plans" (e.g., California Department of Alcohol and Drug Programs 1985).

This approach to prevention has important implications and special problems for Mexican Americans. To the extent that they are included in local-level group processes that result in regulatory policies, they can influence policy in such a way that it is responsible to their unique cultural needs. It would be possible, for example, for Mexican American communities to address the problem of excessive numbers of liquor outlets in areas of heavy Mexican American population concentration (Burns 1983). However, age, legal status, and economic and language factors frequently limit Mexican American participation in community action. Further, Mexican American subpopulations are very differently integrated into larger communities from city to city (Gilbert 1980). In order to make prevention activities of the type described above culturally relevant, a master plan for community initiatives must incorporate mechanisms for assessing ethnic communities' abilities to mobilize around prevention activities. Plans should also include contingency strategies for overcoming obstacles to ethnic group participation.

The kinds of data that inform culturally relevant decision making at the funding and planning levels of the service providing structure are usually archival and survey types of data—not what we usually consider core anthropological data. However, anthropologists familiar with an ethnic group can be of great help to planners in determining the kinds of data needed, directing the collection of appropriate survey and archival materials, and interpreting and contextualizing the data.

Culturally Relevant Program Design

It is at the level of program design that the concept of cultural relevance of services has been most frequently invoked. But it is also in the provision of direct services that the greatest problems are encountered in trying to achieve cultural relevance. One of the difficulties facing those who are charged with designing and providing culturally appropriate services is that they have limited empirical data on specific cultural traits on which to base service designs. The demographic and epidemiological data valuable to policymakers in the ways described above are too general to be useful in the face-to-face interactional contexts of daily service provision. Further, service providers do not have easy access to the data on ethnically distinct cultural traits that appear in scholarly journals, nor have they been trained to look for important interactions between cultural traits or to interpret the significance of these cultural configurations in terms of their *particular* services. All too frequently, the result is a reliance on cultural stereotypes.

Let me illustrate. Familism, defined as strong loyalty to family members and preference for interaction and exchange relationships confined to family members, is noted as being particularly characteristic of Mexican Americans. In numerous papers discussing the provision of services to this ethnic group (e.g., Salcedo 1974; Sotomayor 1971), one finds reference to the uniqueness of the Mexican American extended family as an important mutual aid resource. If a description of the extended family is given, we usually are told that it includes a sizable array of consanguineal and affinal kin and compadres incorporated into closely interacting household constellations. Most of the time very few empirical data are provided for assessing the degree and kind of interaction and exchange usual in these kin groups. Typically, generalized descriptions of the kin group are followed by statements such as this:

> By not understanding and utilizing the kinship system as part of the design of social services and programs, an important resource for addressing needs is lost. [Rivera-Martinez 1985:202]

Unfortunately, in most of these discussions, no concrete suggestions about how the kinship system might be used in addressing specific service-related needs are forthcoming. Many recommendations surrounding the issue of cultural relevancy in service provision are left at this level of generality.

Knowledge of a single, generalized cultural trait, such as familism or extendedness of family, is of little practical value to program planners and service providers. Much more detailed information about an ethnic group's kinship relations needs to be known in order to incorporate kin groups effectively into service delivery strategies. Program designers must consider very carefully the implications of including extended family members in specific program contexts. For example, in the alcoholism field, planned interventions which are counselor-advised confrontations between family members and alcoholism have come into therapeutic vogue as a strategy for getting abusive drinkers into treatment. Family systems treatment modalities are also important in long-term counseling with alcoholics and their families. How will these family-oriented approaches have to be modified in order to reflect sensitivity to Mexican American family patterns in light of the familistic cultural trait? One might expect that the intervention or family therapy groups might be larger than would be the case with Anglo Americans since extended family members might be included. However, other ways in which the familism of Mexican Americans is expressed need to be considered in this *specific context.* Would, for example, members of the *drinker's* extended family, cousins and brothers, who also happen to be members of the alcoholic's long-term drinking group, be included? Research indicates that working class Mexican American males are more likely to have family members as regular drinking companions than Anglo males (Gilbert 1984, 1985). How should the counselor work with the information that the man does a considerable portion of his drinking at family-organized and -sanctioned celebrations, a cultural pattern noted among Puerto Ricans (Aguirre-Molina 1979)? Clearly, it is not just the fact of an extended family that is important here but a whole array of significant issues that surround the expression of familism in a particular cultural group.

Obviously, too, the meaning and salience of unique cultural traits, such as norms governing family and gender roles, will vary in terms of the kinds of services being considered. In the context of maternity services, for example, the more segregated male/female roles found among rural immigrant Mexican husbands and wives may suggest to a childbirth educator that she should be as accepting of female relatives as birth coaches for Mexican women as she is of husbands in that role for her Anglo clients. The educator will have to consider what advantage or disadvantage she would be conferring on her Mexican-born client if she urges the husband's "egalitarian" participation as in the middle class Anglo model. Perhaps such urgings will simply result in the couple's failure to complete the series of classes. Taking another example, the alcohol treatment counselor who must make a decision whether or not to include an immigrant client's wife and children in support groups has other issues to consider concerning ethnically specific role relations. The nontraditional incorporation of wife and children in a man's affairs would seemingly undercut the authority of the recovering man's family roles. Will the benefit of enhanced family interaction which could accompany the family's participation in support groups offset the threat to the man's authority during a time when he is already suffering from lowered self-esteem?

Intra-ethnic variation in a culturally important trait such as family extendedness also might affect services to a specific target population. Research based on empirical measures of mutual aid exchange in Mexican American extended families shows that the degree of such aid varies considerably in terms of the economic and generational status of family members. And existing data also show that those Mexican American families most likely to need helping services, i.e., poorer or immigrant families, are also least likely to have supportive naturally occurring kinship groups (Keefe and Padilla 1987). Certain other segments of this ethnic population lack particularly strong kin ties. For instance, Markides and Mendes de Leon, after a careful study of Mexican American and Anglo elderly in an urban setting, concluded that "Mexican American elderly were no longer advantaged in the extended family structure as compared to the Anglo elderly" (1987:153). Mexican Americans have a considerably higher rate of female-headed households than is the case in the larger population—what impact does this have on extended family functioning? Differences such as these will certainly affect the manner and the degree to which service providers working with certain subsegments of this ethnic population can incorporate kin groups in their service delivery plans.

Opportunities for Anthropologists

I have seen little in print or in the planning of service providers that acknowledges the complexity of the issues I have raised here. Furthermore, I have seen little in the writings of applied anthropologists to interpret their findings in the context of specific service-related needs. My illustrations have centered primarily on one ethnic group and service field, but the need for culturally relevant approaches is apparent in many of the service fields and for many ethnic groups.

Applied anthropologists are especially well equipped for meeting the challenge of achieving cultural appropriateness in human services. Some of us have been lucky enough to have done research in the countries from which U.S. ethnics or their families derive and have potentially useful insights. In this respect, we occupy a unique position among applied social and behavioral scientists. We are also experienced in the development of richly detailed concrete data gathered in natural settings (as opposed to survey, experimental, or laboratory studies). Furthermore, we have been trained to interpret the meanings of specific behaviors and traits in terms of total cultural complexes.

We need to expand our skills in order to increase our professional visibility and make policymakers and service providers aware of our potential for enhancing the cultural appropriateness of services. First, many of us need to broaden our knowledge base about specific service-providing arenas that can use the information we have. We need to be able to separate the many bureaucratic levels of the service-providing structure and recognize the functions of each so that we can communicate our particular data to the most responsive ears. Learning something of the language and culture of different service arenas also would improve our communication. In order to make concrete, programmatic recommendations, we will need to couch them in terms familiar or at least understandable to persons outside our discipline. For example, the term "emic" has much to do with cultural relevance but may be rejected as incomprehensible anthropological jargon by service providers.

We need to consider more carefully how to interpret our data for use in specific strategies and actions to be taken in discrete service arenas. All too often in our executive summaries, reports, and articles, we are concerned only with theory, explanation and description. The practical implications of our theories and findings are frequently summarized in a couple of sentences in our conclusions, often with the expressed (or unexpressed) hope that others will do the hard work of translating our data into designs for action. We need to be well informed about the services that could potentially use the information so that *we* can take this final step toward application.

We can increase our participation in activities such as conferences, training activities, and policy making where we can make our culturally sensitive data directly available to persons who can use it. This means that we may want to present findings at local and national conferences that draw together practitioners in the fields we hope to impact: health educators, clinicians, doctors, substance abuse specialists, nurses, urban planners. Additionally, we will find receptive audiences in the readership of journals and publications directed to specialized service fields. Finally, sitting on boards and commissions that oversee planning and resource allocations is another way of making our expertise in cultural issues available to decision-makers.

Note

Acknowledgments. Support for the preparation of this paper was made available through Grant No. R01-AA07363 from the National Institute on Alcohol Abuse and Alcoholism.

References Cited

Aguirre-Molina, Marilyn
1979 Alcoholism and the Hispanic Woman. Paper presented at the Women in Crisis Conference, New York.

Burns, Marcelline B.
1983 The Alcohol Problem in Los Angeles. Abstracts and Reviews in Alcohol and Driving 4(4):9–15.

Caetano, Raul C.
1987 Alcohol Use Among Hispanic Groups in the U.S. Working paper F-214. Alcohol Research Group, 1816 Scenic Ave., Berkeley, CA 94706.

Caetano, Raul C. and Maria Elena Medina-Mora
1986 Immigration, Acculturation, and Alcohol Use: A Comparison Between People of Mexican Descent in Mexico and the United States. Working Paper No. C-46. Berkeley: Alcohol Research Group.

California Department of Alcohol and Drug Programs
1985 Framework for Community Initiatives. Preventing Alcohol Problems in California, 1985. Sacramento: California Department of Alcohol and Drug Programs.

Giachello, Aida L.
1985 Hispanics and Health Care. *In* Hispanics in the United States: A New Social Agenda. Pastora Cafferty and William C. McCready, eds. New Brunswick: Transaction Books.

Gilbert, M. Jean
1980 Communities within Communities: Minority/Majority Relations in Three California Communities. Hispanic Journal of Behavioral Sciences 2:241–268.
1984 Social Epidemiological Factors Underlying Contrasts in Mexican American and Anglo American Blue- and White-Collar Drinking Patterns. Paper presented at the annual meeting of the American Anthropological Association, Denver.
1985 Mexican Americans in California: Intracultural Variations in Attitudes and Behavior Related to Alcohol. *In* The American Experience with Alcohol: Contrasting Cultural Perspectives. Linda Bennett and L. Ames, eds. New York: Plenum Press.

Gilbert, M. Jean, and Raul C. Cervantes
1987 Alcohol Services for Mexican Americans: A Review of Utilization Patterns, Treatment Considerations and Prevention Activities. *In* Alcohol and Mexican Americans. M. Jean Gilbert and Raul C. Cervantes, eds. Los Angeles: Spanish Speaking Mental Health Research Center, University of California, Los Angeles.

Keefe, Susan E., and Amado M. Padilla
1987 Chicano Ethnicity. Albuquerque: University of New Mexico Press.
Markides, Kyriakos S., and Carlos Mendes de Leon
1987 Aging, Family Relations and Mental Health: Selected Findings from a Three Generation Study of Mexican Americans. *In* Mental Health Issues of the Mexican Origin Population in Texas. Raymundo Rodriguez and Maria Tolbert Coleman, eds. Austin, TX: Hogg Foundation for Mental Health.
Rivera-Martinez, Carmen
1985 Hispanics and the Social Service System. *In* Hispanics in the United States: A New Social Agenda. P. Cafferty and William McCready, eds. New Brunswick: Transactions.
Salcedo, Consuelo
1974 Mexican American Socio-Cultural Patterns: Implications for Social Casework. San Francisco: R and E Associates.
Sotomayor, Marta
1971 Mexican American Interaction with Social Systems. Social Casework 52(5):316–322.

About the Authors

M. Jean Gilbert received her Ph.D. in anthropology from the University of California, Santa Barbara, in 1980. Her work has included cross-cultural studies in kinship, formal and informal support networks, childbirth, and the social epidemiology of alcohol use. She is currently the National Institute on Alcohol Abuse and Alcoholism Scholar in Hispanic Alcohol Studies at the Chicano Studies Research Center, University of California, Los Angeles. She is presently completing work on two clinic studies focused on Mexican American alcohol treatment clients in which she examines the relationship between alcohol-related cognitions, severity of alcohol involvement, and level of acculturation.

Richard Handler was educated at Columbia University and the University of Chicago, and is Assistant Professor of Anthropology at the University of Virginia. He is the author of *Nationalism and the Politics of Culture in Quebec* (University of Wisconsin Press 1988), and is completing a book on the anthropology of Jane Austen's novels. His current research concerns history museums in the United States.

Susan Emley Keefe received her Ph.D. in 1974 from the University of California, Santa Barbara, and is Professor of Anthropology at Appalachian State University. Her scholarly work has been interdisciplinary and has combined theoretical and applied interests, primarily in ethnicity, mental health, and education. She is the co-author (with Amado M. Padilla) of *Chicano Ethnicity* (University of New Mexico Press 1987) and editor of *Appalachian Mental Health* (University Press of Kentucky 1988). Her current research is on ethnicity as it is expressed among black and white Appalachians and its impact on education and mental health.

Mary I. O'Connor is Assistant Research Anthropologist at the Social Process Research Institute, University of California, Santa Barbara. Since receiving her Ph.D. in anthropology from UCSB in 1980, she has been the consultant for Native American Concerns on numerous environmental impact reports in the Santa Barbara area. She is currently a Fulbright Professor at the Centro de Investigaciones y Estudios Superiores en Antropologia Social in Oaxaca, Mexico.

Gregory G. Reck received his Ph.D. in anthropology from the Catholic University of America. His early research focused on economic and social change in an ethnically plural village in rural Mexico and he is author of *In the Shadow of Tlaloc: Life in a Mexican Village* (Waveland Press 1978). More recently, he has transferred his interests in change and ethnicity to research in Appalachia. He is currently Professor of Anthropology and Assistant Dean for Research and Grants at Appalachian State University.

Una Mae Lange Reck received her Ed.D. from the University of North Carolina at Greensboro with a graduate cognate area in anthropology. Prior to her current work on ethnicity and education in Appalachia, she conducted research on self-concept and self-esteem of rural Appalachian children as compared to urban non-Appalachian children. She is currently Professor of Education and Assistant Dean of the College of Education at Appalachian State University.

To the reader:

Please fill out this form or a copy and give it to your librarian or information center manager.

Dear ____________________ :

I recommend for purchase ___ copy(ies) of *Negotiating Ethnicity: The Impact of Anthropological Theory and Practice* (NAPA Bulletin 8), 1989, Susan Emley Keefe, ed., $7.50, available from:

National Association for the Practice of Anthropology
American Anthropological Association
1703 New Hampshire Avenue, NW
Washington, DC 20009

Sincerely,

____

(Date) ____________________ (Title) ____________________

---

napa bulletins

Why are anthropologists joining together in local practitioner organizations? What do anthropologists in government agencies do? How does one set up and operate a research and consulting business?

These are some of the questions answered in recent issues of the NAPA Bulletin, a monograph series for practitioners in the social sciences published semiannually by the National Association for the Practice of Anthropology, a Unit of the American Anthropological Association.

The following issues are now available:

1 Directory of Practicing Anthropologists
H. Max Drake, Roger D. Karlish, and Ann M. Drake, comps.
$4.50 (members), $6.00 (nonmembers)

2 Business and Industrial Anthropology: An Overview
Marietta L. Baba
$4.50 (members), $6.00 (nonmembers)

3 Becoming a Practicing Anthropologist
John van Willigen
$3.00 (members), $4.00 (nonmembers)

4 Research and Consulting as a Business
Nancy Yaw Davis, Roger P. McConochie, and David R. Stevenson
$4.50 (members), $6.00 (nonmembers)

5 Mainstreaming Anthropology: Experiences in Government Employment
Karen J. Hanson, ed., John J. Conway, Jack Alexander, and H. Max Drake
$5.50 (members), $7.50 (nonmembers)

6 Bridges for Changing Times: Local Practitioner Organizations in American Anthropology
Linda A. Bennett
$6.00 (members), $7.50 (nonmembers)

7 Applied Anthropologist and Public Servant: The Life and Work of Philleo Nash
Ruth H. Landman and Katherine Spencer Halpern, eds.
$6.00 (members), $7.50 (nonmembers)

8 Negotiating Ethnicity: The Impact of Anthropological Theory and Practice
Susan Emley Keefe, ed.
$6.00 (members), $7.50 (nonmembers)

Please include payment, in U.S. funds, with all orders.

American Anthropological Association
1703 New Hampshire Avenue, NW
Washington, DC 20009